THE PUFFIN

MAHABHARATA

THE PUFFIN
MAHABHARATA

NAMITA GOKHALE

Illustrated by

SUDDHASATTWA BASU

PUFFIN BOOKS

To all my grand nieces and nephews, and to my beloved nephew Jaidev,
and all the other children, both young and old, in my extended family

PUFFIN BOOKS

Published by the Penguin Group
Penguin Books India Pvt. Ltd, 11 Community Centre, Panchsheel Park, New Delhi 110 017, India
Penguin Group (USA) Inc., 375 Hudson Street, New York, New York 10014, USA
Penguin Group (Canada), 90 Eglinton Avenue East, Suite 700, Toronto, Ontario, M4P 2Y3,
Canada (a division of Pearson Penguin Canada Inc.)
Penguin Books Ltd, 80 Strand, London WC2R 0RL, England
Penguin Ireland, 25 St Stephen's Green, Dublin 2, Ireland (a division of Penguin Books Ltd)
Penguin Group (Australia), 250 Camberwell Road, Camberwell, Victoria 3124, Australia
(a division of Pearson Australia Group Pty Ltd)
Penguin Group (NZ), 67 Apollo Drive, Rosedale, North Shore 0632, New Zealand
(a division of Pearson New Zealand Ltd)
Penguin Group (South Africa) (Pty) Ltd, 24 Sturdee Avenue, Rosebank, Johannesburg 2196, South Africa
Penguin Books Ltd, Registered Offices: 80 Strand, London WC2R 0RL, England

First published in Puffin by Penguin Books India 2009

Text copyright © Namita Gokhale 2009
Illustrations copyright © Suddhasattwa Basu 2009

ISBN: 9780143330486

Typeset in Perpetua by Abha Graphics, New Delhi

Printed at Singapore

I begin by paying homage to Ganga,
and to the Himalayas, the source of the river and
all the stories that spring forth from it. The book
celebrates the river Yamuna, by the banks of which
Lord Krishna played and sported. It is in memory
of the ancient city of Indraprastha, the heart of
which still beats under the skin of modern Delhi. It
is written with reverence for the dusty fields of
Kurukshetra, where in the thick of battle Krishna
explained the laws of karma to his kinsman Arjuna.
It is dedicated to the land of Bharata, which renews
its past with every living moment. And to the next
generation of readers, who continue to remember
and retrieve the stories of an enduring culture, as
they dream once again of Jaya, the song of victory.

C O N T E N T S

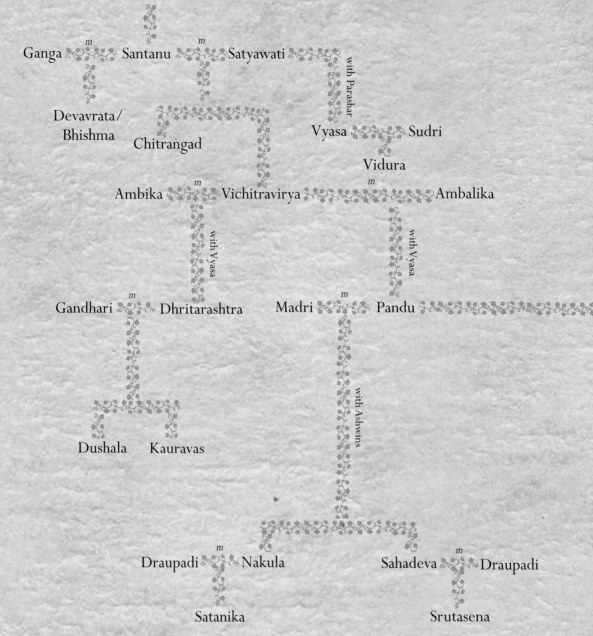

Bharata

Ganga —m— Santanu —m— Satyawati —— with Parashar

Devavrata/
Bhishma

Chitrangad

Vyasa —— Sudri

Vidura

Ambika —m— Vichitravirya —m— Ambalika

with Vyasa

with Vyasa

Gandhari —m— Dhritarashtra

Madri —m— Pandu —m—

with Ashwins

Dushala   Kauravas

Draupadi —m— Nakula

Sahadeva —m— Draupadi

Satanika

Srutasena

Family tree as per the text

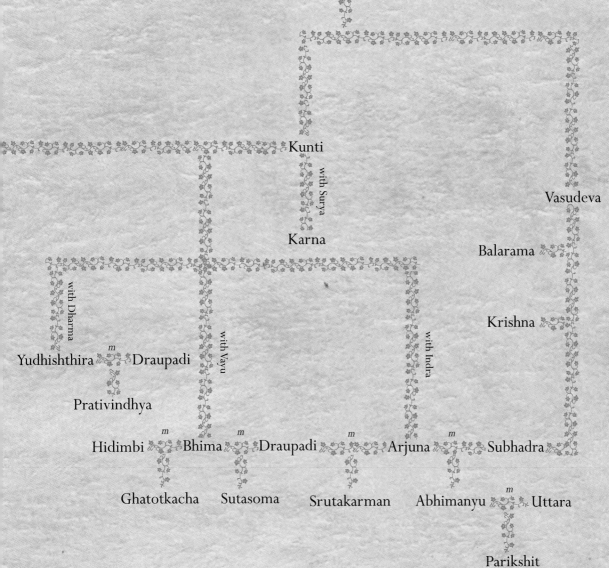

Surasena

Kunti with Surya

Karna

Vasudeva

Balarama

Krishna

with Dharma

Yudhishthira *m* Draupadi

Prativindhya

with Vayu

with Indra

Hidimbi *m* Bhima *m* Draupadi *m* Arjuna *m* Subhadra

Ghatotkacha   Sutasoma   Srutakarman   Abhimanyu *m* Uttara

Parikshit

Janamejaya

JAYA

THE STORY OF THE MAHABHARATA

Along, long time ago, in the ancient lands of India, known in those days as Bharatvarsha, a family quarrel grew into a bloody war. There had been wars before, and there have been wars since, but that mighty battle between warring cousins of the Kuru clan has become a part of the mythology and history of India. Told and retold a million times, the story of the Mahabharata is about defeat as well as victory, humility as much as courage. It is the greatest story ever told.

There are four cycles of time that rule our universe, which are known in Sanskrit as the four yugas. These are the Satya, the Treta, the Dwapara and the Kali yugas. The Mahabharata war was fought at the very end of the Dwapara yuga. And as the heroic Pandavas began their last journey, to find their place in heaven or in hell, the Kali yuga of our present, mortal times began.

It was almost three thousand years ago, in what is now northern India, that the Kuru kingdom flourished by the banks of the river Yamuna. It was here, in the city of Hastinapura and in nearby Kurukshetra, that the great battle was fought. The kings and princes who are the heroes of the tale were all descendants of King Bharata, and so it is known today as the Mahabharata. However, in the beginning it had a simple title and was known only as the 'Jaya', the song of victory.

Generations have told each other this story. Parents have repeated it to their children, teachers have narrated it to their students. It was recited out loud by bards in royal courts and sung by wandering minstrels as they travelled through the land.

The sage Vyasa, son of the sage Parashar, was one of the immortals who could live forever, defying the laws of time. He had heard the Mahabharata from many different narrators and had himself played an important role in the turn of events before the beginning of the actual battle. He decided one day to write down the story of this grand battle and preserve it for posterity. He wrote it in the language of those times, which was Sanskrit. And he wrote it in verse, so that it would be easy to memorize and recite.

All this was, of course, before the age of printed books. There was no paper as we know it today. Writing is never easy, but it was even more difficult in those days, when people had to make do with palm-leaf manuscripts and reed pens. The story Vyasa set out to tell was also complicated beyond belief, with tales within tales, so that one could sometimes lose the thread of the main story. He knew that he had taken on a daunting task and decided to get the blessings of Brahma, the Creator of the world.

Vyasa prayed to Brahma to grant him the strength and talent to record the story of the Mahabharata. Brahma appeared before Vyasa and blessed him. 'But how can I tell this great tale alone without any help or support?' Vyasa wondered aloud, still a little discouraged by the difficulty of the undertaking. Brahma, who knew of events past and present and those yet to come, nodded wisely. 'Ganesha, the elephant god, is famous for his learning and memory,' he said. 'Pray to Ganapati Ganesha. He alone can help you.'

So Vyasa prayed again, and as Brahma had promised, the elephant-headed god appeared before him.

'I will help you, O sage' Ganesha replied to Vyasa's request. 'But on one condition. I insist that my pen must not stop even for a moment while I write down the Jaya, the song of victory. You must not halt or pause when telling the tale, and I too will write it down in one continuous flow.'

Vyasa thought for a while. He knew that the help of Ganesha meant that he could tell the Mahabharata in a way that his readers could understand and remember. 'I agree,' he said finally. 'But I too have a condition. You, Ganapati, must listen carefully while I tell of the Jaya and make sure that you have understood everything completely before you write it down.' Ganesha smiled and nodded his great trunk to indicate his acceptance.

So the two got to work together. It took many, many years. Sage Vyasa would compose verses and Ganesha would write them down. Day and night they sang and wrote the Jaya, until finally it was done and ready, told for all time.

But the thing about stories is that they are never finally told. They are always retold

and rewritten, in new tongues, new languages, for new times, even as I am retelling it to you now. Just so, Narada, the messenger of the gods, recited the song of victory to all the great immortals in heaven and earth who had not heard it before. Suka, son of Vyasa, sang it to the sprites and spirits and demons, the gandharvas, the yakshas and rakshasas who inhabited the different worlds and dimensions. The story was also told to Vaisampayana, who was a student and disciple of Vyasa.

Many years after the time in which the battles of the Mahabharata were fought, Janamejaya, the son of King Parikshit who ruled the Kuru kingdom between the Saraswati and Ganga rivers, held a grand public sacrifice. Here, amidst the chanting of prayers, the story of his ancestors was told all over again by Vaisampayana.

In the audience, listening intensely, was a young storyteller named Suta. The story made a deep impression on him. As Suta grew older, he travelled far and wide, visiting all the places mentioned in the tales of valour and sacrifice told by Vaisampayana. He saw for himself the mountains and rivers, the battlefields and sacred places, and he pictured in his mind how things had been so many, many years ago. Then Suta called all the sages and wise men of his age to the forest of Naimasa. Under the shade of leafy trees, he retold the story he had first heard as a young boy.

It is Suta's Mahabharata that I will retell. The story of the Pandavas and the Kauravas, the hundred and five brothers and cousins who grew up playing the same games, learning from the same teachers. They studied the art of war and trained as warriors together. Yet they were very different in the way they understood the rules and philosphy of battle, and years later they stood against each other in war. The Mahabharata is the grand epic of their lives, and of their ancestors and their descendants. There are stories within stories in it, each with a word or lesson for those who can spot it. And at the core of the story, like the seed in a fruit, is the Bhagvad Gita, where Lord Krishna and his friend Arjuna discuss the big questions of life.

But to tell this properly, we will have to begin at the beginning, and go even further back in time.

THE GODDESS GANGA

Perhaps it all began with the river goddess Ganga, who had come down to earth in human form and was beautiful beyond belief. King Santanu of Hastinapura, the ancestor of the Kauravas and the Pandavas, saw Ganga and instantly fell in love with her. 'Marry me and become my queen,' he pleaded.

Ganga, being an immortal, knew and understood the dangers of marrying a mortal. 'It cannot be!' she exclaimed. 'Our love can only lead to disaster.'

'I do not know who you are, but I will marry only you!' King Santanu insisted.

The king pleaded and protested until Ganga finally agreed to become his queen, but on one condition. 'Never ask me who I am,' she said, 'or where I come from. Never question anything I do, good or bad. Accept me as I am, and I shall be yours. But if you question me, or judge my actions in the light of your own understanding, I shall be compelled to leave you.'

The king was so madly in love with Ganga that he agreed to everything. They were married and lived together happily.

The time came for Ganga to bear the king a child, the heir to his kingdom. The little baby was born amidst great rejoicing, but to the king's absolute horror, the queen took her firstborn and cast him into the Ganga, the river which bore her name. The child fell to his death, drowning in the swirling waters, while Ganga watched on, smiling inscrutably.

Santanu remembered the strange promise he had made to Ganga before marrying her and did not question his wife on why she had killed their child.

This happened again and again and again. Each time Ganga had a child, she killed it by drowning the innocent babe in the river. Seven times Ganga bore Santanu a son and seven times the king watched on helplessly as she murdered him.

The eighth time, as she was about to cast the child into the water, Santanu grabbed her by the arm and stopped her. He snatched the wailing child and held him tight. 'This child must live!' he exclaimed. 'I cannot allow you to kill him!'

Ganga looked sadly at her husband and child. 'Santanu, I know my strange actions have puzzled and pained you,' she said, 'but I had my own reasons for acting as I did. I must leave now, for you have broken your promise. But before I go, I will tell you why I was compelled to kill our sons.'

Santanu listened, amazed, as Ganga told him the story. 'There was once a holy man called Vashishta, who owned a beautiful and magical cow. The eight Vasus, the gods of the elements, visited the mountains with their wives. On the way up they passed the hermitage where Vashishta lived. One of the Vasus, Prabhasa, loved his wife so dearly that he could refuse her nothing. She saw Vashishta's cow and asked Prabhasa to steal it for her. He agreed, and the other Vasus helped him with the theft. They took the cow and its calf away from the hermitage and continued on their journey as though nothing much had happened.

'Vashishta came to know of this through his magical powers. He was furious and cursed all the eight Vasus, who belonged to the world of immortals, that they would be born as mortals in the world of men.

'The very worst thing that can happen to us immortals is to be forced to live in the human world,' Ganga explained to Santanu. 'The Vasus begged and pleaded for mercy but Vashishta could not take back his curse, even though he had begun to feel a bit sorry for them. He agreed to soften the curse and promised that the seven Vasus who had merely helped Prabhasa to steal his cow would leave the human world as soon as they were born into it and return to the world of the immortals. Only Prabhasa, who had wilfully planned the theft, would be condemned to live out an entire lifetime as a human before he could return where he truly belonged.'

The king listened to his wife, their little baby held protectively in his arms. 'The Vasus came to me for help,' Ganga explained. 'They begged me to become their mother in the human world and to kill them as soon as they were born. I have now fulfilled this duty. But alas! You have broken your vow to ask me no questions and now we must part.' She took the little child from the king and disappeared into thin air before his eyes.

Santanu was left all alone to rule his kingdom and remember his days of happiness with his mysterious wife.

Many years passed. One day, as Santanu was walking along the banks of the Ganga, thinking as he often did of the wife who had left him, he saw a handsome young boy playing among the waves. The child held a bow and arrow in his hands and was furiously taking aim at the waves, building a dam across them with his arrows. In a flash, King

Santanu understood that this must surely be his son, born of the river goddess Ganga. He called the boy to his side and looked into his eyes.

At that very moment, Ganga herself materialized before him. 'You are right, Santanu,' she said, smiling as though reading his thoughts. 'This is none other than our son Devavrata. He has studied in the world of immortals, where he has been taught the arts of war and archery by the brave master of weaponry Parshurama, and the learning of the Vedas by holy Vashishta. He has been instructed in the great sciences by the learned sage Sukra. The time has at last come for you to take our son back and rear him in the world of humans.'

With these words Ganga disappeared once again, leaving the wondering king to reflect on the inexplicable tricks of fate, destiny and the gods.

 SATYAWATI

King Santanu announced that his son Devavrata would succeed him as king, after his death. Devavrata was crowned the Yuvaraja, the royal heir, amidst much rejoicing in a grand ceremony in Hastinapura. Four years passed in happiness and contentment.

One fateful day, Santanu was walking by the banks of the Yamuna river. Suddenly, the air was filled with a delightful fragrance. The puzzled king searched for the source of the lovely scent. He saw a beautiful maiden standing bashfully beside a boat by the bank of the river. Instantly he fell in love with her, just as he had done with Ganga so many years earlier.

This maiden was Satyawati, the daughter of the Chedi king Uparichara, the chief of the fisherfolk, who had found her in the belly of a large fish. She was very beautiful, but always carried about her body the distinct smell of fish. When she was very young, the sage Parashar fell in love with her. He took her in a boat to a mysterious island, and with his magical powers, removed the smell of fish from her. Instead, the sweet fragrance of flowers clung always to her body. Parashar and Satyawati had a son, who was born on the river island. Parashar took his son, who later became the poet Vyasa, to a forest hermitage, while Satyawati returned to her father's kingdom.

It was Satyawati, fragrant as flowers, whom Santanu sighted, as she stood by the river bank.

'Who are you?' Santanu exclaimed, and then almost in the same breath, 'Will you marry me?'

'I am Satyawati, the daughter of the king of the fishermen,' Satyawati replied with a radiant smile. 'I ply this boat between the banks of the Yamuna, taking passengers from one shore to the other. If you wish to marry me, you must first ask my father for his permission.'

The infatuated king rushed to meet Uparichara, chief of the fisherfolk. 'I am Santanu, king of Hastinapura,' he said. 'I could smell a wonderful fragrance by the banks of the Yamuna and followed it until I found your beautiful daughter. I have fallen in love with her! I want to make her my wife!'

'My daughter is as noble as she is beautiful,' the king of the fishermen replied. 'A great sage granted her the boon that she would spread fragrance wherever she goes. Yes, I will give my daughter to you in marriage, King Santanu, but there is a condition you must fulfil.'

'I will do whatever you wish,' King Santanu said impatiently. 'What is it you want?'

Uparichara cleared his throat and looked Santanu in the eye. 'My daughter's son should be the king after you,' he said.

Santanu was speechless. He thought of his beloved son, Devavrata, whom he had crowned as his heir. He could not be so unjust as to deprive Devavrata of the throne. Without a word, he left the king of the fisherfolk and rode back to Hastinapura.

DEVAVRATA'S VOW

After Santanu returned to the palace, he tried his utmost to forget the beautiful, sweet-smelling fisher-maiden he had fallen in love with. But try as he would, he could not forget her. Haunted by her memory, he crept around his palace, sad and restless, a shadow of his former self.

Devavrata noticed the change in his father. 'Why are you so sad, Father?' he asked repeatedly, but the king would say nothing. When Devavrata persisted, he answered him indirectly. 'You are my only son,' he said. 'As a king, it is my duty to see that my family line does not die out. A king must have many sons, for a king's life is uncertain, and wars and enemies are the way of life for a king's son. If anything were to happen to you, who would rule the kingdom after me?'

Devavrata was too intelligent to be fooled by such evasive statements. He questioned the king's charioteer and came to know the story of his father's frustrated love for the fisher-maiden. Where other sons may have felt threatened at the prospect of their father remarrying, Devavrata was only full of sympathy for his father's dilemma. 'I must help my father,' he resolved.

Devavrata went to meet the king of the fishermen. 'Please allow your daughter to marry my father, King Santanu,' he entreated.

Uparichara listened politely to Devavrata. 'I would gladly do as you say, honoured prince,' he said, 'but I have already made my condition clear. My daughter deserves not only to become the queen of King Santanu, but also the mother of the future king. As you have already been anointed the crown prince by your father, my daughter's children, my grandchildren, can never inherit the throne and the kingdom.'

Devavrata listened patiently to this outburst. 'I will do anything for my father's happiness,' he replied. 'I give you my word that I shall never aspire to inherit the throne or the kingdom. The son born of your daughter shall be crowned king when the time comes. I renounce all my rights as my father's eldest son to be his heir apparent, if that can persuade you to let your daughter marry my father.'

The chief of the fishermen was astounded by the young man's generosity and lack of greed or pride. However, he was still not completely satisfied by Devavrata's reply. 'I am sure that you fully mean what you say at this moment,' he said, 'but what of the future? You are a hero, the pride of the Bharata race; your sons too will be heroes like you. What if they are unhappy with your decision to renounce the throne? They may declare war on my grandchildren and seize the kingdom by force! A man must look ahead when he plans his daughter's future.'

Devavrata thought for a while before replying. 'There is only one way out,' he said at last. 'I vow that I shall never marry or have children. I promise to renounce the joys of a wife and family. I shall live a life of celibacy forever so that I have no sons who can challenge your grandsons' throne.'

It is not easy for a young man, and a crown prince at that, to be so unselfish. As the gods and immortals heard Devavrata make his vow (for they can hear anything, anywhere and at any time), they were struck by his resolve. 'Bhishma,' they cried as they applauded him and showered flowers upon him from the heavens. 'Bhishma! Bhishma!' 'Bhishma' means someone who has undertaken a difficult vow and cannot be moved from his word. From that moment onwards, until he died many years later at the battlefield in Kurukshetra, Devavrata was known to all as Bhishma.

Santanu was married to Satyawati, princess of the fisherfolk. The royal couple had two sons, Chitrangad and Vichitravirya. Bhishma was pleased to see his father so happy, and his father too was moved by his son's loving sacrifice. In gratitude, Santanu granted him a boon. 'Take these words as my gift,' he said. 'Death will never come to you, O Bhishma, as long as you wish to live. It is only when you decide to die, and when you yourself grant permission to the lord of death to approach you, that your time in this world will be over.'

Santanu retired to a forest hermitage by the banks of the Ganga. Bhishma governed the kingdom on behalf of his two younger brothers, who were too young to rule. Chitrangad was killed in a battle with a gandharva, and his brother Vichitravirya became the heir apparent to the kingdom.

Soon it was time for Vichitravirya to marry and have children to continue the royal line. Bhishma took it upon himself to find a suitable bride for his brother.

THE STORY OF AMBA

It was customary in those days for a princess to choose her husband through a swayamvara. The ceremony would be held at her father's court. Princes and kings from near and far who wanted to marry her would gather to demonstrate their valour and courage, through a test. The princess would garland her chosen suitor, usually the victor, to indicate she was willing to marry him.

It came to Bhishma's notice that the king of Kashi was planning to hold a swayamvara for his daughters, Amba, Ambika and Ambalika. He, too, decided to attend the ceremony. The handsome young princes of Koshala, Pundra, Banga and Kalinga had all come to Kashi to vie for the favours of the beautiful princesses. They were amazed to see Bhishma, who was much older than all of them, at the palace. 'What on earth is this old man doing here?' they asked each other, not realizing that the noble warrior had come to win a bride for his younger brother Prince Vichitravirya. Little did they know that Bhishma was the greatest athlete and archer of his time.

When the time arrived for the contest, Bhishma defeated all the princes with ease and won the three princesses, Amba, Ambika and Ambalika. He set off with them in his chariot, already planning the grand festivities for the wedding ceremony of Vichitravirya.

Amba, the eldest of the three princesses, had made up her mind to marry Salva, the king of the lands of Sambala, and no one else. Salva, too, had fallen hopelessly in love with the beautiful Amba and was dismayed by Bhishma's victory at the swayamvara. Resolving to win back his beloved, he set off in a cloud of dust in pursuit of Bhishma's chariot.

Salva stopped Bhishma's chariot midway to Hastinapura and challenged the great warrior to fight him. Bhishma, who had never been defeated in battle, soon began to get the better of Salva. Amba watched in horror as the two men struggled, with Salva teetering on the brink of defeat. She could not watch him die before her eyes. 'Stop!' she screamed. 'Noble Bhishma, you cannot kill the man I love!'

Kuru warriors were bound by a very strict code of honour. They could not kill an adversary when someone pleaded for his life. Bhishma turned scornfully to Salva. 'You may go,' he said, dismissing him. 'Your life has been saved by a mere woman!' Gathering the three princesses back into the chariot, he set off again for Hastinapura, where Vichitravirya awaited his three brides.

Amba wept bitter tears as the dejected figure of Salva receded behind her. 'My life is ruined,' she sobbed, and Ambika and Ambalika tried their best to console her.

Once they arrived in Hastinapura, the preparations for the wedding began. Amba still could not forget Salva. She confronted Bhishma again. 'I have resolved to marry Salva, not your brother Vichitravirya,' she declared, 'and nothing can ever make me change my mind.'

Bhishma was confused. He was a righteous and just man, who always wanted to be honourable. What was the right course of action? Would it be fair to force the unwilling Amba to marry Vichitravirya?

Finally, Bhishma came to a decision. 'You may marry Salva,' he told Amba and sent her, escorted by handmaidens, in the royal chariot to Salva's kingdom of Sambala.

However, Amba's troubles were far from over. Salva had been angry and humiliated at being defeated in battle by Bhishma while fighting for Amba's favour. 'What are you doing here?' he asked, when she arrived at his palace. 'Bhishma has won you not once but twice: first at your swayamvara at Kashi and then when I challenged him on the way to Hastinapura. You belong to him, not to me. I cannot marry you, now or ever.'

Poor Amba! It was hard being a woman in a world where the menfolk decided on everything that women could or could not do. She returned to Hastinapura and told Bhishma what had happened. 'What should I do now?' she wondered.

Bhishma attempted to persuade Vichitravirya to marry Amba. He had already married Ambika and Ambalika. But Vichitravirya refused. 'She has already given her heart to another man!' he exclaimed. 'It would hurt my honour if I married her now.'

Amba turned to Bhishma. Her lustrous eyes were full of tears. 'If nobody will marry me, you must,' she entreated.

Although Bhishma felt sorry for Amba and was moved by her tears, he could not do as she said. He was bound by the promise he had made to King Uparichara that he would never marry and have children. He was a warrior and he had to keep his vow, whatever the circumstances.

Rejected by Salva, Vichitravirya and Bhishma, Amba felt betrayed and humiliated. She was even angrier with Bhishma than she was with Salva, for she felt that he alone was the cause of her troubles. 'I will take my revenge on Bhishma,' Amba vowed. 'I will be the cause of his death.'

For many years, Amba tried to avenge her humiliation. One by one, she tried to provoke Bhishma's enemies to rise against him, but to no avail. Finally, she turned to Parshurama. She knew that only he had the courage to confront the invincible Bhishma. It was a long and bloody battle, but in the end, Bhishma defeated Parshurama.

Amba was an exceedingly determined person. Consumed with despair and the desire for revenge, she went to the high, snowy Himalayas and meditated and prayed to Lord Shiva (also known as Adideva), the god of all the gods. After many, many years of such austerity, Lord Shiva appeared before her. 'I am pleased with your prayers, Amba! I will grant you whatever boon you please,' he said.

Even after so many years of meditation, Amba had not forgotten her intense hatred for Bhishma. 'I desire only one boon, O Shiva,' she replied. 'I want to be the cause of Bhishma's death, as revenge for his destroying my life.'

The incongruity of the opponents—the mighty warrior against the delicate princess— did not perplex Shiva. He never disappoints those who pray to him sincerely. 'In your next birth, you will surely slay Bhishma,' Shiva assured Amba.

So impatient was Amba to undertake her revenge that she lit a blazing fire and leapt into the pyre to kill herself. Amba was born again as the daughter of King Drupad. She was to grow up into a mighty warrior, and in time, disguised as the male warrior Sikhandin, she was destined to kill Bhishma in battle. But that was yet to be.

Meanwhile, the sisters Ambika and Ambalika were married to Vichitravirya, but the

Kuru king was weak and kept poor health. Soon after his wedding, he died, leaving his wives childless. Their mother-in-law Satyawati mourned for her son and felt desperately sorry for her two young widowed daughters-in-law. Bhishma, too, was worried about the future of the royal family line and the governance of the kingdom.

When Satyawati married Santanu, she already had a son, Vyasa. As was the custom in those days, Bhishma requested Satyawati to ask Vyasa to act as a substitute husband for Ambika and Ambalika so that they might have sons who could govern the land.

Vyasa could not refuse his mother. He lived for a month with Ambika and for another with Ambalika, and then for a third month with Sudri, one of Satyawati's maids. When he had done his duty and fathered three sons, he left again for the forest hermitage where he lived.

When the children were born, Bhishma raised them as his own. Ambika's son, the firstborn Dhritarashtra, was blessed with strength and courage. But he was born blind, and so the kingdom was entrusted to Ambalika's son Pandu. The young Pandu was fair-skinned, but somewhat sickly. The maid's son was named Vidura and brought up by Bhishma with the other two boys.

✦ THE BIRTH OF KARNA ✦

In the nearby kingdom of Pritha, Surasena, the father of Vasudeva and the grandfather of Lord Krishna, had a beautiful daughter called Pritha. As his cousin Kuntibhoja was childless, the young Pritha was given by Sura to be adopted by Kuntibhoja. From that day onwards, she was known as Kunti.

When Kunti was a young girl, the sage Durvasa visited Kuntibhoja. Kunti looked after their holy guest with great devotion. Pleased with her kindness and hospitality, Durvasa gave her a boon. 'I will teach you a secret mantra,' he said. 'If, after repeating this mantra, you call upon any god, he will visit you and give you a son equal to him in glory.'

One day, when Kunti was playing by herself, she saw Surya, the sun god, shining in the heavens in all his glory. Impulsively, she repeated the divine mantra that Durvasa had taught her to summon the gods. At once, the sky grew dark, as the radiant sun god left the heavens and came to Kunti's side. The rays of the sun shone around Surya's head in a glittering golden crown. Long, heavy gold earrings, his kundalas, hung from his ears. His golden armour, his kavach, shone on his body. The sun god was handsome beyond belief.

'Who are you?' Kunti inquired, dazzled by his splendour.

'I am Surya, the sun god,' he replied. 'You called and I have come, to give you a child as strong and valiant as I am.'

'But I have no husband, Lord Surya,' Kunti stuttered in dismay. 'How can I have a son?'

'You have invoked the mantra's power,' Surya replied. 'You must now bear my son. The children of the gods are born in one day. Have no fear, beautiful maiden.'

The next evening Kunti gave birth to a handsome child. He was born wearing golden armour and earrings, and he shone with the splendour of his father, Surya. Afraid to tell her father of what had happened, Kunti placed the child in a straw basket, which she lined carefully to make it waterproof. She took the basket to the banks of the river Yamuna, where she set it adrift in the flowing waters. 'May the river goddess guide you to happiness,' she whispered to the sleeping child. She watched the basket bob downstream until it disappeared into the horizon. Then she returned home and wept to herself, worrying ceaselessly about her abandoned son.

As the Yamuna flowed into the Ganga, the child was safely washed ashore into the hands of a charioteer called Adiratha. Adiratha and his wife were childless, and delighted by the unexpected gift of a lovely baby. 'This is surely the child of a god!' Adiratha exclaimed. 'His armour shines bright as the sun, and his gold earrings radiate a divine splendour. We shall name him Karna and train him to be a mighty warrior!'

The time came for Kunti to be married. Kuntibhoja invited all the kings and princes of the neighbouring states for a splendid swayamvara. Eager suitors rushed to the palace. Among them was Pandu, whom Kunti chose as her future husband by placing a garland of white flowers around his neck. They were married and returned to Hastinapura.

In the meantime, Bhishma, too, had been looking for a bride for his nephew. Quite unaware of Pandu's wedding to Kunti, he promised him in marriage to Madri, daughter of the Madra king Salya. Thus Pandu had not one but two wives. They lived together happily in Hastinapura.

In those days hunting was the sport of kings. One day, Pandu went to the forest for a hunt. A holy sage and his wife were roaming together in the forest, disguised as a doe and deer. As they were making love to each other, Pandu saw them, took aim with his bow and arrow, and shot them. He was of course quite unaware of the real identity of his victims. Both the doe and deer were fatally wounded.

Though still disguised in the form of a deer, the sage spoke in his human voice to curse Pandu. 'Hear my death curse,' he said, even as the last breath was leaving his body. 'For your cruelty in killing me while I made love, I curse you to suffer the same fate! You too shall die when you next sleep beside your wife.'

Pandu decided to retire to the forest and live the life of a holy man, to atone for the sin he had committed accidentally. He urged his wives, Kunti and Madri, to remain at the palace in Hastinapura, but they insisted on accompanying him into exile. 'I am of no use as a king or a husband,' Pandu sighed, 'for I can no longer have children to carry on my line.'

It was then that Kunti confided to him about the boon granted to her by Sage Durvasa. 'You need not despair,' she told Pandu. 'We can still have children. By the power of the mantra Durvasa taught me, I can have children from any god I desire.' Pandu was overjoyed. The first child, Yudhishthira was born of Dharma, the god of justice and righteousness. Their second son, Bhima, was born of Vayu, the god of the wind. Arjuna, the third, was born of Indra, the lord of the heavens.

Madri begged Kunti to let her too use the power of Durvasa's mantra. Kunti, who was always generous and kind, did as Madri requested. Madri invoked the Ashwins, the twin horsemen who are the gods of dawn. She named the twin sons that she bore Nakula and Sahadeva.

THE BIRTH OF THE KAURAVAS

When Pandu left for the forest hermitage with Kunti and Madri, Dhritarashtra was left to rule the kingdom alone. Bhishma sent messengers to the mountain kingdom of Gandhara to ask for the hand of the king's daughter Gandhari in marriage.

Gandhari travelled to Hastinapura with her brother Sakuni to marry Dhritarashtra. She had dreams, as young girls do, of what her future husband would be like. She hoped he would admire her beauty and fall in love with her. It was only after she arrived at Hastinapura that she discovered that her future husband had been blind since birth. But

Gandhari was a very noble and strong-minded girl. When she discovered this, she resolved to blindfold herself all her life long, and share her husband's handicap. And so the young girl from the mountains of Gandhara sacrificed her sight and embraced darkness.

Dhritarashtra grew to love his wife fiercely. When she became pregnant, he impatiently awaited the birth of their child. More than a year passed, and still Gandhari's pregnancy continued. She finally gave birth after two years. A hard ball of flesh emerged from her womb, which was divided into a hundred and one pieces, each of which was placed in a bronze jar filled with clear butter. So in time the hundred and one children of Dhritarashtra and Gandhari came to be born. The first of their sons was named Duryodhana, and the second Dusasana. The remaining ninety-eight were also sons, and the last one was a daughter named Dushala. Their parents, the king and the queen, rejoiced and were content, as they watched their children grow to manhood in the palace grounds.

PANDU'S DEATH

Meanwile, Pandu, Kunti and Madri continued living in the forests, in a hidden valley of the Himalayas, far away from the palace in Hastinapura. They watched with delight as their five sons, the Pandavas, became accomplished young men. The golden-eyed Yudhishthira and his powerfully-built brother Bhima were fair-skinned. The middle brother, Arjuna, was dark, strong and valiant. Nakula and Sahadeva were mischievous and full of fun. In his joy and contentment, Pandu quite forgot the curse that the sage, who had died in the disguise of a deer, had set upon him.

One day, an arrow from the god of love, Kamadeva, fell upon Pandu. He held his wife Madri and caressed her. The sage's curse was fulfilled, and Pandu died in Madri's arms.

Madri was stricken with grief and guilt. She blamed herself for what had happened. Her screams and lamentations rent the skies. 'I don't want to live any more,' she wept. 'I will die with you, beloved husband!' And so the two died, like the sage and his wife before them, so many years ago.

Kunti was left a widow, with five young sons to raise. Two holy men, who were wandering through the forest, found the bodies of Pandu and Madri and cremated them. Then they escorted the weeping Kunti and her five sons back on the long journey to Hastinapura.

Bhishma, Dhritarashtra and Vidura were shattered when they heard the news of Pandu's death. The holy men handed the ashes of Pandu and Madri to Vidura, and left again for the mountains. The rest of the family consoled the grieving Kunti.

KRIPA AND DRONA

As the Kauravas and the Pandavas grew up in Hastinapura, their grand-uncle Bhishma continued to look after them, as he had done with their parents and grandparents before them. He watched over them carefully, guiding them on how to conduct themselves as great warriors and noble kings. But Bhishma knew they needed other teachers. He was eager that the one hundred and five boys—his wards—should learn the art of war and become skilful in the handling of difficult weapons. He searched far and wide for a suitable teacher, and finally appointed Kripa, a skilled archer.

Kripa had been found in the forest, along with his twin sister, during the reign of Santanu. The man who found them, in a bush near Hastinapura, was a Kuru soldier. They were bundled in a deerskin, with a strung bow and arrow beside them. The little boy held on tightly to the arrow and would not let go of it. The soldier took them back to the palace, where he presented them before Santanu. 'They are clearly the children of a Brahmin well skilled in archery,' the king observed. 'I name the boy Kripa and his little sister shall be called Kripi. Let them be raised in my palace from now on.' Kripa grew up to be skilled in archery, while Kripi became a beautiful young maiden. She was married to Drona, the son of the sage Bharadwaja.

Drona grew up in his father's ashram, where the Panchala king had sent his son Drupad to study. The two boys became friends. Then the Panchala king died and Drupad returned to become king in his place.

After Drona married Kripi, they too went to Panchala. They were poor and their son, Ashwathama, had very little to eat or drink. Drona explained to Ashwathama that they were poor and must learn to do without, but such lessons are hard for a little boy to understand. One morning, Ashwathama returned home weeping. All the boys who he played with were used to drinking milk, which was a luxury he had never tasted. They offered him a drink made of white rice-water mixed with water. 'Why don't you taste some milk?' they mocked. Ashwathama danced with joy, believing that the rice-paste he was drinking was milk. Once he finished, the other boys teased him mercilessly.

Ashwathama returned home and wept. Kripi tried to comfort him. Drona too was upset—he felt he had failed as a father. He resolved to visit Kampilya, the capital of Panchala, and meet his childhood friend, King Drupad. He was sure Drupad could help him build a better life.

Drona travelled the long distance from his village to Kampilya and sought an audience with the king. 'Don't you remember me?' he asked the proud Drupad eagerly. 'I am your friend Drona; we played together as children at my father's hermitage.'

King Drupad frowned at Drona with arrogant displeasure. 'I have friends and enemies only among my equals,' he exclaimed. 'You are poor, lazy and unlucky. Don't you dare call yourself my friend!'

Although Drona remained silent after listening to Drupad's rude comments, he resolved in his heart to take his revenge someday. He returned home to Kripi and Ashwathama, and told them it was time to leave the kingdom of Panchala. They left for Kripi's childhood home of Hastinapura.

The Kauravas and the Pandavas were happy to be taught by Kripa. They called him Kripacharya, Kripa the teacher, and treated him with the deep respect due to all teachers.

One day, the five Pandavas were playing with a ball in the fields outside the Hastinapura gates. It fell into a deep, dark well. Though they tried their hardest, they could not get it out.

Just then, Kripa's brother-in-law Drona happened to be passing the city gates. He saw the young princes struggling to extract the ball from inside the well. 'I will help you,' he said.

Drona plucked a handful of durba grass and recited a magical mantra over it. He leaned over the edge of the well and threw in a long blade of grass, which pierced the ball. Then he threw in another, which connected with the first, and then another, until a long chain was formed. Drona pulled the ball out before the astonished Pandavas. 'It's quite easy if you know how to do it,' he told them. 'Watch this.'

Drona took a gold ring from his finger and threw it down the well from which he had extracted their ball. 'Now give me a bow and arrow,' he said. Arjuna, whose favourite sport was archery, promptly did just that. Drona took aim carefully, and his arrow shot into the well, only to speed back at almost the same moment with the gold ring embedded in its head.

'Teach us your skills,' Yudhishthira begged, 'and we will stand by you whenever you need us.'

Drona smiled. 'Take the arrow with the ring on it and show it to your grandfather Bhishma,' he instructed.

When Bhishma heard what had happened from the excited boys, he knew he had found another worthy teacher. He summoned Drona. 'You are an excellent marksman,' he said. 'Who are you and what are you doing in Hastinapura?'

'I am the son of the sage Bharadwaja. My childhood friend King Drupad insulted me because of my poverty,' Drona replied. 'I have come here to live with my brother-in-law Kripa and begin my life anew so that I may some day seek my revenge.'

Bhishma requested Drona to instruct the Pandavas and the Kauravas along with Kripa. 'Teach them your skills and whatever rewards you want will be yours,' he promised.

Drona and his wife Kripi were no longer poor. They settled down happily in the kingdom of the Kurus and their son Ashwathama studied with the young princes. Every morning, Drona would give each prince a jar with a narrow neck and send them to fetch water from the river. But he always gave Ashwathama a wide-mouthed jar, so that he could return earlier than the princes. In the time before the others returned, Drona would teach his son in secret. But Arjuna learnt to use his arrows to draw water from the river and soon he too began to return earlier than his brothers and cousins. As a result of the extra lessons, Arjuna and Ashwathama became more skilled than all the rest.

The five sons of Pandu and the hundred sons of Dhritarashtra grew up happily together in Hastinapura, playing and fighting and then making up again as young cousins often do. Bhima was certainly the strongest of them all, and sometimes a bit of a bully. He would drag Duryodhana and the other Kauravas by the hair and beat them up. As he was an excellent swimmer, he would not hesitate to jump into the river, holding one or the other of his cousins clasped under his powerful arms. He would dunk them underwater and keep them there until they begged for mercy. If they were climbing trees, he would shake the trees and drop them down like ripe fruit. None of these things made him very popular with his cousins, who would mutter darkly about his pranks.

When Dronacharya had finished teaching all he knew to his students, he called them one by one for a final test. As a target, he perched a bird made of straw and cloth high above on the branch of a tree. First, Dronacharya instructed Yudhishthira, the eldest of the Pandavas, to take aim at the bird. 'What do you see?' he asked, after his student had positioned his bow and arrow.

'I see the tree, the bird, the bow, the arrow, my arm and you,' Yudhishthira replied.

'Stand aside,' said Dronacharya and called in Duryodhana, who gave the same reply, as did his younger brother Dusasana, and the ninety-eight after him.

The same question was asked of Ashwathama. He too positioned his bow and arrow, and replied that he could see the bird, the leaves around it, the branches, and then the sky. Dronacharya told him to put down his bow for he was not yet ready to shoot the bird.

At last it was Arjuna's turn to be called. 'Take aim at the bird's head and then let loose your arrow when I instruct you. Tell me, Arjuna, what is it you see?'

'I see the eye of the bird, and nothing else,' Arjuna replied.

Dronacharya rejoiced, for at least one among his students had understood the essence of what he had tried to teach them. 'I have made you the best bowman in all the world! You have learnt well, Arjuna,' he exclaimed. 'Now you may shoot.'

Arjuna effortlessly shot down the dummy bird with his bow and arrow. Dronacharya turned to his other students. 'How you aim your arrow is more important than how you shoot it,' he said. 'Remember this in life and in sport, and you will always be victorious.'

Now that his students had learnt all that he had to teach, it was time for Drona to seek his guru dakshina, the duty owed to a teacher. 'Go to Kampilya,' he told the Kuru princes, 'and bring Drupad, the Panchala king, to me.'

So the young princes of Hastinapura went to fight Drupad.

Drupad, like Drona, had learnt warfare from the sage Bharadwaja and was a brave and brilliant soldier. Duryodhana and the Kauravas, and the four Pandavas, retreated hastily from his onslaught. Drupad turned back laughing, until suddenly Arjuna stood between him and his city, blocking his retreat.

Raining a relentless volley of arrows upon the astonished king, Arjuna took him captive in his chariot. 'Yield to me and do not fear for your life, honoured Drupad,' Arjuna said politely. 'I must take you to Hastinapura, to my teacher Drona.'

So the humbled Drupad stood before his childhood friend Drona. 'Dear Drupad,' Drona said, 'it is time for you to remember your words, for time leaves nothing true forever. One can only have friends among equals. I must take half your kingdom, so that we may be equals, and you may recognize your childhood friend with love, or hatred, as you please.'

'And what of my capital, from where I rule my people?' Drupad asked.

'It is yours,' Drona replied. 'I am a Brahmin, and we Brahmins are not greedy. Our hearts are made of butter, not stone. Let us be friends once again, Drupad.'

At that moment, Drupad had no choice but to agree, but in his heart he swore undying revenge against the man who had humbled him. 'I shall have a son who will slay this proud Drona,' he resolved, 'and a daughter who shall some day wed the noble Arjuna.' But that story shall be told only later.

As the Kauravas and the Pandavas grew up, their childish quarrels escalated into a more serious rivalry. Duryodhana worried about sharing the kingdom with Yudhishthira after the death of his father, Dhritarashtra. He was convinced that Bhima, physically the strongest of the Pandavas, was the cause of all the problems. He believed that if Bhima were out of the way, things would run smoother for him and his brothers.

Duryodhana, along with his ninety-nine brothers, hatched a plot to kill Bhima and throw him into the Ganga. He invited his brothers and the Pandava cousins for a picnic by the banks of the Ganga. They spent the day swimming and holding races against each other. At night, they slept in tents set up beside the river. Duryodhana had secretly ensured that Bhima's food was poisoned. As he lost consciousness, the Kauravas tied him up with wild creepers and threw him into the river. To ensure that his plan was foolproof, Duryodhana had sharp iron spikes planted into the riverbed at the spot where they had decided to throw in Bhima. If Bhima survived the poison, the spikes would hold him down and ensure that he drowned instead.

However, plans, and especially evil ones, have a way of going wrong at the last minute. The sharp iron spikes that Duryodhana had planted on the riverbed were dislodged by the swift current. A poisonous water snake bit Bhima. Its venom counteracted the poison in the food that the Kauravas had fed him. The river Ganga, taking pity on him, washed him safely to a river bank, where he awoke hale and hearty the next morning.

Duryodhana returned to Hastinapura, quite certain that his plan to murder Bhima had succeeded. The following morning, when Yudhishthira worried aloud about his brother's whereabouts, Duryodhana reassured him that Bhima had left for home early in the morning. Yudhishthira had no reason to disbelieve his cousin, but when he returned to Hastinapura, Bhima had not yet come back. His suspicions aroused, Yudhishthira searched the forests and river bank for his brother, but in vain.

In some time, Bhima trudged back to Hastinapura, weary after his adventure at the bottom of the river. He told Kunti and Yudhishthira of the failed plot to murder him. They consulted their uncle Vidura.

Vidura was a wise and cautious man, and he counselled them to keep what had happened a secret. 'If Duryodhana is accused of attempting to kill you, his anger and hatred will increase a hundredfold. It is best to keep your knowledge of the Kauravas' evil plans to yourself for the time being. Your stars, your fate and the gods above will protect you.'

Duryodhana was angry and surprised to see Bhima alive, but there was very little he could do. The venom from the water snake had only increased Bhima's strength further. Duryodhana burnt with jealousy as he watched his cousin grow stronger with every passing day.

THE TEST OF STRENGTH

Dronacharya and Kripacharya chose an auspicious time to hold a public exhibition of their students' skills. The sightless Dhritarashtra and the blindfolded Gandhari were there, as were Vidura, Bhishma and Kunti. Pavilions had been set up around an open ground and there was rejoicing everywhere. An enthusiastic crowd had gathered to cheer their beloved princes. With such young and valiant rulers to defend them, the people of Hastinapura felt safe and protected from their enemies.

Pipes and bugles announced the entry of the Kauravas and the Pandavas into the arena of the games. 'I am a fortunate man, to have such brave sons and nephews,' Dhritarashtra said contentedly, for he felt as great a kinship with Pandu's sons as he did with his own.

The competitions began. Yudhishthira was adjudged the best charioteer. Nakula and Sahadeva matched each other equally in whatever contest they undertook, which would end inevitably in a draw. Duryodhana's face hardened as he watched Bhima manoeuvre his heavy mace with exceptional but careless skill. Arjuna was the darling of the crowds.

His dazzling display at archery won the loudest applause. It was almost as though he were talking to his arrow, which would do whatever he commanded, flying like a bird through the air, to the astonishment of the audience.

Arjuna was about to be declared the winner of the games, when a sound like thunder rent the cloudless sky. A magnificent young man stood at the gate, clapping both his hands in challenge. Karna, Kunti's abandoned child born of the sun god Surya entered the arena. His golden earrings gleamed and glittered, and his shining armour had the emblem of the sun upon the breastplate. Bowing low before Dronacharya, Karna asked for permission to compete with Arjuna, the winner of the games. Of course, nobody realized that the handsome young man with the proud demeanour was actually Arjuna's half-brother!

Karna began a display of his talents. He tossed a heavy mace with natural ease and it became clear to all who saw him that he was stronger than Bhima, the champion of the mace. His skills with the chariot far surpassed those of Yudhishthira. His arrows too sped through the air at the speed of light, establishing clearly to the amazed audience that he was superior even to Arjuna, the master archer.

Duryodhana watched joyfully as Karna defeated the Pandavas in all that he attempted. He was grateful to the stranger in the golden armour for humbling his proud cousins. He saluted Karna and then embraced him.

'I am Duryodhana, prince of the Kurus,' he said. 'I am your friend for life. Ask me for what you wish and I shall grant it to you.'

'I am Karna,' the young man replied. 'I seek only one boon: that I may engage in single combat with Arjuna, the prince of the Pandavas, and defeat him.'

Kunti, the mother of the Pandavas, had recognized her firstborn child from the moment he appeared. Her heart swelled with love and pride, for she was after all his mother. But now, when she saw her two sons about to engage in mortal combat, she was overcome with fear and horror, and fell into a dead faint.

Vidura, who was wise beyond belief and knew all that was to be known, sensed the full gravity of the situation. He sent Kunti's maids to revive her and consulted Kripacharya about what to do next.

Kripacharya addressed the restless Karna, who was still waiting for an answer to his request. 'Before you combat Arjuna, you must reveal your lineage,' Kripa said firmly. 'Only those born of kings, with royal blood coursing through their veins, may challenge the noble Arjuna.'

Karna went pale, for he had no fitting reply for Kripa's words. His adopted father, Adiratha, shuffled uncomfortably in the audience, not knowing what to do. His birth-mother, the royal Kunti, prayed secretly to his father, the sun god Surya, most royal of the royal, to save their son from this humiliation, even as she longed for the victory of her favourite child, Arjuna.

Duryodhana entered the fray. 'Where do you come from?' he asked Karna. 'Which is your hometown?'

'Anga,' replied Karna, his golden skin flushed with anger and humiliation.

'I appoint you prince of Anga,' Duryodhana declared. 'I seek nothing in return but your friendship.'

From that moment on, Karna pledged his life, his loyalty and his undying friendship to Duryodhana, who had saved him from such public disgrace. His foster father, Adiratha, came forward and touched Karna's feet in homage.

Bhima bellowed with mocking laughter. 'A mere charioteer's son can never become a prince,' he exclaimed scornfully. 'The high-born Arjuna would not demean himself by fighting someone of your humble origins!'

Duryodhana rose once again to his new friend's defence. 'Courage and valour, and not birth, are the hallmarks of a hero,' he said reprovingly.

'It is true that my father is only a charioteer,' Karna said to Duryodhana, 'but he has taught me to be proud and brave. Today, you have honoured me and made me prince of Anga. I shall never forget what you have done for me.'

Meanwhile, the sun had set. Kripacharya stepped forward. 'It is evening,' he said. 'The time for the games is over. You may all disperse and return home.'

And so it was that the battle between the two greatest heroes of the day was postponed until another time.

Duryodhana's envy and hatred of the Pandavas grew every day. He thought them vain, conceited and insufferable. Their popularity with the people of Hastinapura only made matters worse.

Gandhari's brother Sakuni, who had come with her to the Kuru court at the time of her marriage to Dhritarashtra, had stayed on as a royal counsellor. Sakuni was always provoking his nephew Duryodhana to plot and intrigue against the Pandavas.

'I wonder who will rule the kingdom after you? Will it be me or my cousin Yudhishthira?' Duryodhana would ask his father, as though the thought had only casually crossed his mind. Dhritarashtra was in his way a fair man and he did love his nephews, but he doted beyond belief upon his own sons, especially Duryodhana.

'Although you are their king, the people remember that Pandu was chosen king before you. They look at Pandu's sons and think them the future heirs of your kingdom,' Duryodhana would say to his father. Slowly his words began to have effect. Dhritarashtra's love for his nephews began to change into suspicion.

When Duryodhana suggested that the Pandavas be persuaded to leave Hastinapura for a while, Dhritarashtra agreed readily. He requested Yudhishthira and his brothers to visit Varanvata for the festival of Shiva. The Kauravas, especially Duryodhana, went out of their way to praise the beauties of Varanvata. It was decided that the five brothers and their mother Kunti would leave together on an appointed day for the long trip to the north.

Once he managed to persuade his cousins to go to Varanvata, Duryodhana set about executing the evil plan he had so carefully hatched. He and his brother Dusasana ordered their minister, Purochana, to rush to Varanvata and build a beautiful house for the Pandavas, which was to be ready by the time they arrived. This house was to be built of wax and lac, straw and dried wood, and other such materials that could quickly catch fire. 'This house should catch fire in a moment, but nobody should know by looking at it,' Duryodhana instructed Purochana. 'It must have only one door, and no other exit. Your room, Purochana, should be next to the door, so that you can ensure that these accursed five are unable to escape when the time comes for them to die.'

Purochana went to Varanvata with his assistants and set about constructing a splendid palace, built cunningly of all kinds of inflammable material. He built his own room next to the main door, and awaited the arrival of the Pandavas and Kunti.

Duryodhana and his friends were discussing their next move. 'The Pandavas will soon die,' he exulted. 'Then I shall be the crown prince without any challenges, and king after my father dies. Nobody will ever suspect that I had any hand in their murder. Even if they are suspicious, no one will dare to oppose me, for my power shall be all-encompassing.'

And so Duryodhana, Dusasana, Sakuni and their minister Kanika, made plans about how to seize power in the kingdom. 'Bhishma will at worst be neutral, for he loves his family too much to take sides. Ashwathama is my friend, and so his father Drona and uncle Kripa will always be there on our side. As for our uncle Vidura, who may perhaps love our cousins more than he does us, Vidura is no warrior and has no army to back him. How can he possibly harm us?' And so the Kauravas made their plans and daydreamed of the time when the Pandavas would all be dead, burnt to cinders in the wax palace at Varanvata.

But walls have ears, especially in palaces, where servants and courtiers and spies can eavesdrop and overhear the most secret of conversations. Vidura came to know of Duryodhana's plans and grieved that his brother Dhritarashtra and his sons had forgotten all notions of what is right and what is wrong. He remembered his beloved brother Pandu, who had died young, and vowed to himself that he would do his utmost to protect Pandu's widow Kunti and her unsuspecting sons.

When the Pandavas set off for Varanvata, Vidura rode with them part of the way to give them company, and so that he might speak to them in private and warn them of the plot to murder them. He spoke to Yudhishthira in a rough mountain dialect, which the princes had learnt as children when they lived with their father Pandu in the high mountain valley. Vidura knew that none of the other courtiers knew or understood this mountain tongue, and so no one present could understand his intentions. To further protect himself and his nephew, Vidura spoke in riddles, for he trusted that the wise Yudhishthira would be able to decipher their secret meaning.

'All sharp weapons are not made of steel,' Vidura told Yudhishthira, who listened

closely. 'The enemy of water cannot hurt those whose homes have secret doors and passages underground. The blind man never knows where he is going, but one who is forewarned can see even in the dark and find his way with the help of the stars. Take care, my child, and heed my words.'

'I have understood well what you are saying,' Yudhishthira replied. Resolving to look after his mother and his brothers and protect them against any mishap, he set off for Varanvata, while Vidura turned back to Hastinapura.

That evening, when they were resting in the forest, out of earshot of their retinue of servants, Kunti asked her son what it was that Vidura had said to him in the mountain dialect.

'The house we go to is to be set on fire. Uncle Vidura warned us to seek escape through a secret tunnel.' So Kunti and her family were prepared for the evil plot that had been hatched against them.

Purochana was awaiting them when they arrived in the mountain village of Varanvata. The preparations for the Shiva festival were on in full swing. A magnificent palace had been constructed to house the royal visitors. Wood, jute oil and fat had been used to build it so that it would burn easily. The walls had been plastered from the outside, but inside they contained straw soaked in combustible fat. Inviting stools and chairs had been placed in the most dangerous spots. It was a deathtrap, a disaster waiting to happen. But the Pandavas, forewarned by Vidura, did not in the least betray their suspicions.

Purochana watched with malicious delight as the brothers and their mother pretended to admire their new home. 'What lovely curtains!' they exclaimed, although the fabric had been cleverly woven from a special mountain reed that catches fire almost by itself. The floors were covered with loose flintstones, which could spark into flame just by friction. 'I must compliment you on the beautiful stone tiles on the floors,' Yudhishthira told Purochana, who smirked to himself at the Pandava's stupidity.

Bhima was as usual the most impatient. 'We must kill Purochana and make our escape,' he exclaimed. 'I can smell the wax and lac on the roof and the walls; I see the straw, the dry bamboo and reeds behind the plaster. Why are we wasting precious time?'

'You must understand strategy, brother,' Yudhishthira

cautioned him. 'Duryodhana has money and power. His father is blinded by love for him. When the moment is right, we will escape, not before or after. Until then, we shall keep our knowledge of the enemy's plans a secret.'

THE PANDAVAS' ESCAPE

Purochana was certain that the Pandavas had no clue about his evil plans. He dreamt about the rewards that Duryodhana would heap upon him, and felt happy.

In the meanwhile, a miner, who spoke the rough language of the north, came to visit the Pandavas. He sought an audience with Yudhishthira. 'Your uncle Vidura has sent me,' he said. 'You must make plans to escape. In fourteen days, the sun will shine at midnight and you may perish in its flame. Tell me what to do.'

'Begin your digging some distance from the river,' Yudhishthira instructed him, 'and build a secret tunnel which will end in this room, at the very spot where you are now standing.'

'On the afternoon of the thirteenth day, you may raise the boards,' the miner replied.

On the fourteenth day, Kunti organized a sumptuous feast for her attendants and the villagers of Varanvata. At midnight, after everyone had drunk and eaten to their hearts' content and most of the guests had left, Bhima went to Purochana's room, while Yudhishthira proceeded to open the mouth of the tunnel.

'Duryodhana's orders must be obeyed,' Bhima told Purochana. 'The palace must be set afire tonight.' With these words he slammed shut the door to Purochana's chamber and locked it from the outside. He took a torch and set the house on fire. The evil minister was burnt to death, perishing as a result of his wicked plot.

Yudhishthira had already led Kunti, Nakula, Sahadeva and Arjuna down the tunnel. Bhima rushed after them, running for his life even as the wax palace became a molten ball of bursting, crackling flames.

As they fled down the secret tunnel, they could feel the heat of the fire overhead. They groped along in the dark, holding on to each other. When at last the Pandavas stepped out into the windy night, they stared up in amazement at the incandescent sky. It was ablaze with light reflected from the fire.

The wax palace burnt furiously for a few days. The villagers of Varanvata tried desperately to control the fire, but the palace had been constructed with such inflammatory material that it was impossible to extinguish it.

MOURNING IN HASTINAPURA

The news reached Hastinapura. Although Duryodhana and his brothers were overjoyed that their plans to murder their cousins had succeeded, they pretended nevertheless to be heartbroken by the news.

The citizens of Hastinapura were not taken in by the Kauravas' tears. The Pandavas had always been more popular than the Kauravas because of their kind and courteous behaviour. The people muttered their suspicions under their breaths, but none would speak them aloud for fear of the wicked Kauravas.

When at last the flames subsided, the remains of Purochana, along with those of several others, including five young men and a woman, were found among the ashes. The Pandavas had of course escaped, and the bodies belonged to a family of beggars who had come to eat at the royal feast. The Kauravas, however, were now convinced that they were finally rid of their cousins and rivals for the throne.

The first step in evil-doing is always the most difficult. Although Duryodhana was thrilled that he had managed to eliminate his cousins, his conscience did sometimes secretly prick him. After all, he and the Pandavas had all grown up together.

The blind king Dhritarashtra was also battling with conflicting emotions. He grieved deeply at the death of his brother's wife and children at the hands of their own kinsmen, but he knew this would bring peace for his adored, self-willed sons. 'With trust and kindness between us, we could have been like a grove of tall trees in the sunlight,' he thought to himself. 'But now my Duryodhana stands alone, like a single tree in a village square.'

Some of the courtiers noticed that Vidura, who had always doted on the Pandavas, was not as overcome by grief as he might be. 'Is it because he is a philosopher that he can accept the death of his nephews so calmly?' they wondered. Vidura was, of course, secure in the knowledge that the five had survived the fire. The miner who had dug the tunnel through which they had escaped had already reported to him that they were safe and sound. So Vidura tried his hardest to look sad, while in his mind's eye he followed the Pandavas' journey.

Bhishma was heartbroken. Sacrificing his own life and throne, he had guarded and looked after the welfare of his family ever since Santanu had chosen Satyawati as his second wife. Vidura comforted his grand-uncle. 'They are alive still,' he told Bhishma, 'and shall return to claim their kingdom when the time is ripe.'

In a forest far away, the Pandavas wandered, seeking refuge. The brothers were exhausted, and Kunti was overcome by fear and anxiety. Bhima, always the strongest, carried his mother on his shoulders, and Nakula and Sahadeva on his hips, even as he supported Yudhishthira and Arjuna with his arms.

At last, they reached the river where the miner had kept a boat and boatman waiting for them. 'Your uncle Vidura has sent you a message,' the boatman said. 'He warns you not to be careless, and he reassures you that your destiny will never betray you. Let none know your real identity.'

The Pandavas and their mother Kunti crossed the river through the still night. At dawn, they stepped ashore in the heart of a wild forest, far from any town or city. They slept under the trees, exhausted from their long journey. Later, disguising themselves as wandering priests, they made their way through the forest, searching for a place where they could live.

HIDIMB AND HIDIMBI

The forest the Pandavas had found refuge in was called the Hidimbavan. It belonged to a rakshasa called Hidimb, who lived there with his sister Hidimbi. Rakshasas love the taste of human flesh, and Hidimb and Hidimbi would eagerly await the arrival of any man or woman foolish enough to enter their forest, so that they might make a tasty meal of them.

Hidimb was sitting atop a high tree when the smell of human flesh wafted towards his enormous nostrils. His eyes scanned the forest until they rested upon the Pandavas, who were sleeping under the trees. Kunti lay curled up beside them.

Hidimb was feeling rather lazy, so he persuaded Hidimbi to kill the humans and roast them until they were nicely done. Now Hidimbi was a sweet-natured sort of demoness and she agreed immediately to her brother's suggestion. Leaping from tree to tree, she arrived at the spot where the tired travellers were sleeping, unaware of the danger awaiting them.

When Hidimbi saw the sleeping Bhima, with his enormous muscular body, lean hips and wrestler's thighs, she fell instantly in love with him. While Hidimbi was beautiful by demon standards, she knew that this would not appeal to human eyes. She used

her rakshasi powers to transform herself into the most beautiful maiden possible. She now had large, expressive eyes, with thick eyelashes that she batted incessantly, and an enchanting dimpled smile.

Through the mist of sleep, Bhima heard her approaching the spot where he lay. He opened his eyes and saw the lovely apparition, and immediately he too fell in love with her. 'I love you,' Bhima said to Hidimbi. 'Who are you and what are you doing alone in this dark forest?'

'I am Hidimbi,' replied the demoness. 'My brother Hidimb loves the taste of human flesh and wants to eat you for dinner. But I have fallen in love with you—I must save you and your family!'

Bhima was afraid of nobody and nothing. 'I can take your brother on anytime!' he exclaimed.

While Hidimbi and Bhima were busy falling in love, Hidimb had got tired of waiting for his dinner and came in search of his sister. When he heard her talking to Bhima, he flew into an enormous rage. 'I shall kill both of you and eat you up together,' he roared.

'Don't make so much noise, or you will wake my mother!' responded Bhima, and attacked the mighty rakshasa. Hidimb put up a good fight, and the two wrestled and grappled with each other before Hidimbi's terrified eyes.

Kunti and the other Pandavas woke up from all the shouting. Kunti saw the beautiful maiden and mistook her for a forest spirit. 'Are you the guardian spirit of these wild woods?' she inquired. 'And who is this ugly demon who dares to fight my son Bhima?'

Hidimbi told Kunti of her love for Bhima. 'And this uncouth rakshasa who is attacking your handsome son is unfortunately my brother Hidimb,' she said.

The other Pandavas tried to help their brother Bhima, but he pushed them away. Very soon, he had the advantage over Hidimb, and he beat and pummelled and jumped on him until the rakshasa was dead. Hidimbi watched with tears in her eyes; her sorrow at her brother's death was overcome with tears of joy and relief that Bhima was still alive.

'I want to marry you,' Hidimbi said to Bhima. 'I have chosen you for my husband.'

'I love you too,' said Bhima. 'But my brothers and I are wanderers, and I cannot promise to spend the rest of my life with you.'

'Whatever time we spend together will make the rest of my life worthwhile,' replied Hidimbi. 'Marry me! I shall look after you and your mother and brothers like a true and loyal wife, and shed no tears when the time comes for you to leave.'

With Kunti's permission, Bhima married Hidimbi. They lived together in the woods near the sacred lake of Salivahana.

After seven months had passed, the sage Vyasa came to visit them. 'It is not wise for you to rest for too long in the same place,' he advised them. 'Soon Hidimbi will bear you a noble son. After you have blessed him, it will be time for you to move on. You must go next to Ekachakra, for that is what your destiny demands.'

Hidimbi soon gave birth to a son, whom the brothers named Ghatotkacha. He was the favourite of his father, but even more so of Yudhishthira, who spent all his time playing with his little nephew.

Soon their time in Salivahana was up. Kunti and her sons wept many tears at the prospect of leaving Ghatotkacha behind, with only Hidimbi to look after him. But the brave rakshasi kept her word and did not weep a single tear, although her heart was broken at the prospect of being parted from her beloved Bhima.

'Look after our son,' Bhima told her. 'I shall always be with you in my thoughts. Whenever you need me, just think of me and I will arrive by your side.' Yudhishthira held Ghatotkacha in his arms and blessed him, and then it was time for them to begin their wanderings again.

By nightfall, they arrived at the desolate village of Ekachakra, where a few poor huts huddled around the neglected fields. They slept in the open. In the morning, when the village gates were opened, a kind Brahmin invited them to shelter in his house, and they accepted his offer gratefully.

VAKASURA

The Pandavas settled down to their new life in Ekachakra. Disguised as Brahmins, they would beg for food and alms from pious households. Whatever food and money they got would be given to their mother Kunti, who would divide it equally among her five sons. That was how they began; but then the brothers noticed that the mighty Bhima seemed always to be hungry and irritable. They realized that he needed more food than the rest of them put together. Kunti began dividing the dinner into two equal portions: one half for Bhima and the other half to be shared by the rest.

One day, when only Kunti and Bhima were at home, they heard the sounds of loud weeping from the room of their host. Concerned and worried, Kunti rushed to find out what had happened.

The Brahmin, his wife and their children were all sobbing uncontrollably. 'Time and again have I told my wife that we should leave this accursed village of Ekachakra!' the Brahmin lamented. 'A man-eating rakshasa called Vaka rules over this place. Every year, we must send him tribute. He demands a cartload of cooked rice, two buffaloes and an innocent human being to feast upon in a field outside the village. Every year we draw lots to decide who is to be sent to be devoured by Vakasura. Tomorrow is my turn to be eaten alive! What will happen to my family? Who will look after my wife and children after I am gone?' He fell to weeping again.

'I will go in your place, and you can marry once again after I am dead!' his wife volunteered bravely.

'No, let us go,' the Brahmin's children pleaded. 'It is the duty of a child to sacrifice his life for his parents!'

Kunti overheard this conversation. She was moved by their love, and their willingness to sacrifice their lives for one another. 'Wipe your tears,' she said calmly. 'None of you shall die. Send my son to Vakasura. It is the rakshasa's time to die, and my son shall kill him.'

The Brahmin's mouth was agape with fear and astonishment. 'No one can kill Vakasura,' he sobbed, shuddering helplessly as he spoke. 'He is stronger than anyone and everyone. Besides, your son is my guest. It is my sacred duty to protect him.'

'No one in this world can be stronger than my beloved son,' Kunti responded with deep conviction. 'He is invincible in battle.'

When Bhima heard Kunti's plan, he grinned happily to himself. 'I shall have a fine feast tomorrow!' he said, drumming his belly in anticipation.

The next day, the villagers cooked the rice and kept the buffaloes ready. As the wagon departed for the field outside the village, Bhima sat down in it, instead of his host. The other Pandavas, especially Yudhishthira, were worried about their brother but Kunti reprimanded them. 'You are warriors,' she said firmly, 'even though you are now disguised as priests. It is your duty to protect the weak and the helpless.'

When Bhima arrived at the clearing outside the forest, he built an enormous fire upon which he roasted the two buffaloes which had been sent as tribute to Vakasura. The smell of roasting meat spread through the forest, and Bhima got to work eating the two buffaloes. He burped loudly and began on the mounds of cooked rice. In between mouthfuls he would bellow out to the demon. 'Come out, you ugly monster!' he screamed. 'Let's see what you look like!'

Vakasura smelt the roasted meat, and the rice, and the human being full of fresh tasty blood. His mouth watered at the thought of the delicious meal that awaited him. As he strode into the field outside Ekachakra, his good humour turned into rude shock and his eyes popped out of their sockets in surprise. 'Who dares to eat my dinner?' he growled unpleasantly.

Vakasura was tall as a cliff, with flaming red hair and a beard to match. His skin was green, his mouth brown and smelly; his fangs were caked with dirt and blood. As he rushed towards Bhima, he was a truly fearsome sight. But the strongest of the Pandavas smiled unconcernedly and continued to eat the rice.

Vakasura could not bear to watch his dinner disappear. He uprooted an enormous tree and chucked it at Bhima, who brushed it aside as though it were a blade of grass. 'It's bad manners to disturb your guests at mealtimes,' he chided. Vakasura foamed with rage. Bhima ignored him and continued to eat until he had finished every last grain of rice. Then he rose with a sigh of contentment and confronted the angry rakshasa.

'Thanks to you, I've had a decent meal,' he said. 'But that's no reason for you to stay

alive.' He lifted Vakasura high over his head and dashed him to the ground. The demon howled and yelped with pain, and tried to strangle Bhima even as he lay dying. Not for nothing had Kunti described her son as the strongest man in the world! Vakasura was no match for him. He spewed out a fountain of blood from his mouth and uttered a last blood-curdling yelp before he died.

The villagers heard his howls and screams and huddled together in fear, wondering what calamity would befall them next. Even Yudhishthira, Arjuna, Nakula and Sahadeva were worried, though they tried their best not to show it. Only Kunti was not anxious, for she knew her son and how strong he was.

At last, the mighty Pandava returned to Ekachakra, dragging Vakasura's corpse behind him. He left the body at the village gate, and returned quietly to his mother and brothers, for Bhima had to continue to conceal his identity and maintain his disguise as a Brahmin priest.

The next morning, when they discovered Vakasura's mangled body, the villagers stared at it in disbelief. Once they realized that the demon was really and truly dead, their shock turned to joy and relief.

'Who has delivered us from this evil?' they wondered.

'A wandering Brahmin heard my prayers and came to my rescue,' the Pandavas' host replied. 'We are saved forever from the curse of the evil demon Vakasura.' The Pandavas and Kunti smiled mischievously at one another but kept their secret safe and secure in their hearts.

DRAUPADI'S SWAYAMVARA

Ever since the day he had been defeated in battle by his childhood friend Drona, King Drupad of Panchala had been planning an elaborate revenge. He left his queen and palace at Kampilya, and spent his time in prayer and meditation. Every morning, in his prayers, he asked the god Shiva for a son who would defeat Drona.

At last, Shiva came to Drupad in a dream and instructed him to build a fire, into which he was to pour two cups of ghee—one for a son, the other for a daughter. Thus it was that Dhrishtadyumya and Draupadi were born. Dhrishtadyumya came to earth clothed in shining armour, wearing a crown and holding a drawn sword. His sister, Draupadi, stepped out of the fire, radiant and beautiful, with long black hair and sparkling bright eyes. Drupad embraced his two fire-born children. Thanking Lord Shiva for his blessings, he left for Kampilya.

When Arjuna had captured the king on behalf of Dronacharya, Drupad had observed the young Pandava's courage and courtesy. 'This prince, and none other, shall be my son-in-law,' he had resolved. As Draupadi grew into a beautiful young woman, Drupad desired above all else that she should one day marry Arjuna.

As the time for Draupadi's swayamvara arrived, all the kings and princes of the neighbouring states resolved to visit Kampilya for her swayamvara, to try to win Draupadi's bridal garland.

The five Pandava princes, still disguised as Brahmins, were also passing through southern Panchala at that time. Kunti urged them to take part in the contest. 'You are undoubtedly the bravest warriors in the world,' she told them. 'So what if you are in the guise of priests! The rule is that anybody of high birth may try his luck at a swayamvara.'

So the Pandavas travelled to Kampilya. The capital was filled with excitement. King Drupad had ordered a special bow, so strong and stiff that only the greatest of archers could possibly draw it. As a further test of skill, the King of Panchala set up a contraption of revolving wheels and placed a fish within it. The contestants had to aim through the wheels at the fish. But that was not all! King Drupad had decreed that the archers could view the target only through the reflection in the pool below.

The swayamvara began. Dhrishtadyumya entered the competition grounds holding the enormous bow and five long arrows. His sister Draupadi walked behind him, the garland of white flowers for her future husband held in her hands. Royal attendants followed to string up the fish above the pool of water.

Dhrishtadyumya addressed the audience. 'The victor, and my sister's future husband, is he who can string this bow and shoot these five arrows into the eye of the fish,' he announced, pointing to the target that swung this way and that in the breeze.

One by one, the noble kings and princes from near and distant lands rose to try their luck. Many could not lift the heavy bow, and others could not manage to aim it right. Some were even thrown off their feet in the attempt and fell to the ground, covered with dust, as the jeering crowds laughed and ridiculed them. The Kaurava princes too had come for the swayamvara. Duryodhana tried his hand but without success. As one after the other the suitors failed to string the bow, King Drupad wondered if his daughter would ever get married.

At last there were no more kings or princes left. The only other young man besides Arjuna who could have won the contest was his half-brother Karna. But Karna, although he had been born of the sun god Surya and appointed king of Anga by Duryodhana, was still in the eyes of the world the son of a charioteer, and he knew that Drupad would consider him too low-born to marry his daughter. And so Karna had not competed in the contest.

Arjuna observed the beautiful Draupadi from the Brahmins' enclosure where he sat disguised as a priest. 'I must try to win her,' he told himself, and rose to enter the arena. Some of the unsuccessful suitors, who had failed to string the bow, began to jeer. 'He is but a priest,' they said, 'a Brahmin who has spent his life studying and praying! How does he imagine he can find the strength to even hold that heavy bow?'

Dhrishtadyumya silenced them. 'My sister will marry anyone of a good family who can bend the bow and hit the target,' he said. He bowed politely towards Arjuna and urged him to begin.

Arjuna strung the bow with assured ease, and looked around him at the expectant crowd with a mischievous smile. He lowered his gaze and stared intently at the reflection of the fish in the pool of water. Then, before the audience in the arena had the time even to blink, he had shot the five arrows into the eye of the fish.

The princes and kings were shocked by the unexpected skill of this unlikely priest. They stared in disbelief as Arjuna approached the princess Draupadi, even as the other Brahmins jumped and shouted in exultation, waving their deerskins in an excited victory dance.

Draupadi stared shyly at her future husband, noticing how handsome and valiant he looked. She glowed with joy and happiness as she garlanded him with the white flowers.

Some of the disgruntled princes and rejected suitors were eager to pick up a quarrel. 'A king's daughter cannot marry a priest!' they exclaimed. 'We shall not allow it.' Krishna, the son of Kunti's brother Vasudeva, was there too, along with his brother Balarama, and they tried their best to calm things down. Bhima, rough and ready as always, uprooted a medium-sized tree from the ornamental garden and stripped it of its leaves so that he could use it as a makeshift bludgeon. Arjuna threw a dusty robe around his new bride, and rushed her out of the arena. He commandeered a waiting chariot; the charioteer was too intimidated by Bhima's menacing bludgeon and enormous physique to refuse their request. And so it was that the princess Draupadi came to be married to the same Arjuna who had kidnapped her father so many years ago, just as Drupad had hoped.

The brothers arrived home, where Kunti was anxiously awaiting their return. Dhrishtadyumya followed them secretly. When he saw the five brothers with their regal-looking mother, he was convinced that they were none other than the Pandavas and Kunti. He rushed back to Kampilya to tell his father the good news.

'I have brought home a precious gift today, mother,' Arjuna announced, as he introduced his new bride to Kunti.

Kunti had always urged her sons to share everything equally. 'Then you must share it with your brothers,' she replied.

Arjuna turned to his new bride, 'I have always obeyed my mother, and shared everything with my brothers,' he told the bewildered Draupadi. 'Now I must share you, my wife, equally with them. You shall be wife to all of us five brothers, and we shall all give you our love and honour and protection.'

A few days later, Drupad called Arjuna and Draupadi to Kampilya. He was a bit surprised and confused that Draupadi was by now married to all the five brothers and that he had not one but five sons-in-law! He gave the Pandavas his blessings, and promised to help them get their kingdom back, so that his beloved daughter could rule as queen.

The news of Draupadi's swayamvara reached Hastinapura. Vidura was overjoyed and rushed to Dhritarashtra's royal chamber to give him the news. 'King Drupad's daughter has become our daughter-in-law,' he exclaimed. 'Our kingdom will be strengthened with such powerful allies!'

Dhritarashtra immediately, and quite naturally in the circumstances, assumed that his favourite Duryodhana had triumphed at the swayamvara. 'Bring Draupadi before me,' he said excitedly. 'The princess of Panchala has been wise in choosing my dear Duryodhana.'

Vidura hastened to correct his mistake. 'It is Arjuna who has won the princess of Panchala,' he explained. 'Our brother's sons are alive, and the five Pandavas have jointly married Draupadi. They are now in Kampilya, accompanied by Queen Kunti, living under the protection of King Drupad.'

Dhritarashtra was extremely upset by this news, but he could not betray his true feelings. The failed plot to murder the Pandavas had to remain a secret at any cost. 'I am delighted at this unexpected news,' the blind king murmured, screwing up his face into an unconvincing expression of joy. 'How absolutely wonderful! And here we were mourning their deaths!'

The news that the Pandavas were alive, and married to the daughter of King Drupad, spread through the palace like wild fire. Some of the courtiers were overjoyed, but most of them were cautious in displaying their emotions. The eldest of the Kaurava brothers, Duryodhana and Dusasana, rushed to their uncle Sakuni in consternation. 'We should never have trusted that fool Purochana,' Duryodhana whispered, gnashing his teeth as he spoke. 'Fortune has favoured the Pandavas again. They have escaped death by fire, and survived to emerge stronger than ever, with Dhrishtadyumya and Sikhandin to strengthen their camp. We must destroy them speedily before we perish at their hands.'

This Sikhandin that Duryodhana spoke of was a mighty warrior with a strange history. When Princess Amba had been scorned by Bhishma, who had refused to marry her, she had sworn revenge and won Shiva's blessing that she would succeed in her goal in her next life. Determined to avenge her humiliation Amba decided to kill herself so that she could be reborn and seek her revenge. She was reincarnated as Sikhandin, the daughter of Drupad. When she was still young, she found a garland of never-fading flowers that Amba had placed as a challenge to Bhishma. By a prediction of Parshurama, whoever wore this garland was destined to kill Bhishma. The young princess Sikhandin had confidently placed the still-fresh garland around her neck.

King Drupad was alarmed that a mere girl, vulnerable and defenceless, was presuming to fight the great Bhishma. Women warriors were still unheard of in those days. 'It cannot be,' he exclaimed, 'you are a mere woman, not a warrior!'

So Sikhandin was sent into exile to repent and mend her ways. Sikhandin prayed and meditated until she assumed the guise of a man. Then she, or rather he, studied the art of war and became a famous and fearless soldier, accomplished in every aspect of battle.

Duryodhana was determined to resist the Pandavas' return. Accompanied by his loyal friend Karna, he went to Dhritarashtra's chamber and sought his father's counsel.

'Do not speak of these matters before Vidura,' the blind king warned his eldest and favourite son. 'You must not display your disappointment at the Pandavas' good fortune in front of him. Whatever we do must be done secretly and under the guise of brotherly affection.'

Consumed with envy, Duryodhana proposed a series of improbable plans. 'Let us create enmity among the five Pandavas,' he blustered, 'and break their unity. Or, we could bribe Drupad to take our side against his sons-in-law.'

'Don't be foolish, Duryodhana,' Karna said, with his customary bluntness. 'The Pandavas have seen through your machinations. It will not be so easy to fool them now. The only honourable way out is through warfare. We must strike on the battlefield and destroy them with our superior strength and skill.'

Dhritarashtra consulted with Bhishma, the patriarch of the family, as well as with their guru Dronacharya. Both agreed that the Pandavas should be invited back to Hastinapura and given their share of the Kuru kingdom. Dhritarashtra secretly resented this good advice. He believed his adored sons deserved to inherit the entire kingdom. But he could not show his true feelings, and had to put up a pretence of agreeing with them. 'My nephews shall have the share in the kingdom that my brother Pandu left in trust with me,' he said, trying his hardest to sound sincere.

Duryodhana, Dusasana and Karna listened to these words in consternation. They were young and in a hurry to prove themselves. Bhishma and Drona's words of wisdom, drawn from a lifetime of experience, struck them as being weak and defeatist.

Vidura was dispatched to Kampilya, the capital of Panchala, to invite Kunti, the Pandavas and Draupadi back to Hastinapura. His chariot was loaded with gifts of jewels and fine robes for King Drupad, Draupadi and the Pandavas.

Vidura was thrilled to see his beloved nephews, whom he had protected since childhood. Queen Kunti and the Pandavas were moved to tears at being reunited with the person who had stood by them through all their adversities. However, all of them, including Drupad, were rather suspicious of Dhritarashtra's invitation. 'I don't trust him one bit,' Kunti confided to Vidura. 'And with good reason! But you have our trust. We owe our lives and all we have to you. We shall do as you advise.'

'You must come to claim your kingdom,' Vidura told the Pandavas. 'You are protected by the gods, and by your own righteousness and good conduct. You have nothing to fear; it is time for you to return with me to Hastinapura.'

And so the Pandavas returned to their own land. King Dhritarashtra followed Bhishma and Drona's advice and gave the Pandavas their share of the kingdom near the Khandava forest by the river Yamuna. The ancient ruined city of Khandavaprastha, which had once been destroyed by the ancestors of the Kuru dynasty, was part of their share and they resolved to establish their capital there. Yudhishthira was crowned king. Duryodhana could scarcely contain his rage, but he was helpless and compelled to tolerate this most unwelcome development.

◂◖ INDRAPRASTHA ◗▸

Queen Kunti was the daughter of Sura, who had given her to his cousin Kuntibhoja to adopt. Krishna, who had by now become very close to the Pandavas, particularly Arjuna, was King Sura's grandson. Being Kunti's nephew and cousin to his new friends made Krishna's bond with the Pandavas even stronger.

Krishna was the king of the Yadavas, and his beauty, intelligence and charm drew everybody who met him like a magnet. Was Krishna a man or a god? Nobody was really sure. But what was well established was that he was the world's mightiest warrior, and a good friend and adviser to the Pandavas. With King Drupad and his sons Dhrishtadyumya and Sikhandin, and Krishna as their allies, the Pandavas were now more powerful than they had ever been.

The land around the ancient ruined city of Khandavaprastha was a desolate waste with no plants or trees, birds or animals in it. But the Pandavas, assisted by Krishna, were determined to make the wasteland bloom into a great city. An auspicious day was selected by the astrologers to begin the reconstruction. The great sage Vyasa arrived to give his blessings, to the accompaniment of holy incantations. The celestial architect, Vishwakarma, appeared and began to work his magic. The gardens flowered again, the lakes were once more brimming with water, and lustrous lotus blooms floated on them. The forts and palaces were reconstructed and looked more beautiful than they had ever done. The Pandavas named their new capital Indraprastha. People came from far and wide to admire its glory, and the brothers reigned in peace and prosperity.

Soon after they moved to Indraprastha, Arjuna accidentally broke a promise he had made to his brother Yudhishthira. Nothing was more sacred to a Kuru warrior than his word, and so Arjuna decided to go into exile for a year as penance.

Disguised as a holy man, Arjuna set off on his long pilgrimage. He visited all the sacred rivers, the holy Ganga which flows from the Himalayan mountains, the Godavari and Kaveri rivers in the south. He travelled along the sea coast until he reached the western ocean near Dwarka. This was the city where Krishna ruled jointly with his brother Balarama. As children, Krishna and Balarama had lived by the river Yamuna near Mathura with their foster parents, the cowherd Nanda and his wife Yashoda. They were in hiding from their evil uncle Kamsa, who constantly plotted to murder them. When they came of age, they claimed their kingdom again.

Since he was a young child, Arjuna had heard stories of the beauty of Krishna's sister Subhadra. When he arrived at Dwarka, dressed like a wandering monk, covered in ashes, he lost his heart to the princess. Of course, he was already married to Draupadi, as were his brothers, but things were different in those times from what they are now, and he decided to marry Subhadra as well. She too had heard stories of her handsome and heroic cousin Arjuna since her childhood and was already half in love with him. They received Krishna's blessings and returned to Hastinapura. Draupadi was not too pleased at first, but Subhadra won over her new family with her goodness and kindness. Krishna and Balarama came laden with gifts to celebrate her wedding. Balarama soon returned to Dwarka but Krishna stayed on to spend time with his favourite cousins.

THE KHANDAVA FOREST

One day, as Arjuna and Krishna were walking by the edge of the Khandava forest, they saw a tall, lean Brahmin who looked as though he were starving. 'Can we get you something to eat?' they inquired, worried that he might die of hunger.

'Yes, you may!' the lean man replied, smiling strangely as he spoke. 'I am Agni, the lord of fire, and I wish to devour this forest.' Fire is always hungry. Agni was bored of all the ghee and clarified butter fed to him at the sacrificial fires lit in his honour. 'I want to get my teeth into some hot, crackling trees!' he exclaimed. 'And since you offered to get me food, you must help me burn this forest. It is guarded by a snake called Takshaka, who is a great favourite of Lord Indra. Every time I set fire to the forest, Indra sends a shower of rain to put it out. I knew when I saw the two of you that you were sent to help me.'

A warrior must stand by his word, and so Arjuna and Krishna resolved to help Agni, the lord of fire, to devour the Khandava forest. But how would they do that? 'We have no weapons with us here,' said Arjuna.

Agni summoned Varuna, who promptly appeared to present a magnificent bow to Arjuna, along with two quivers full of magical arrows that could never be exhausted. The bow was called Gandiva and was famed through the three worlds for its invincible powers. No warrior who owned it could ever meet with defeat.

Arjuna knelt low before the mighty bow and saluted it reverentially. It was the most wonderful gift he had ever received. He strung the bow, and the string sounded with a sharp twang that echoed through the forest.

Next, Agni gave Arjuna a white chariot, with four white horses yoked to it that flew faster than the wind. A flag with the emblem of the monkey god fluttered atop the chariot.

To Krishna, Agni presented a chakra, a razor-sharp discus with a thousand spokes and an iron rod through the centre, from which to throw it. 'This is the Sudarshan Chakra,' he explained. 'It is the deadliest weapon ever to be conceived. It has always been yours through births and rebirths. I was only holding it in trust, but the time has arrived to return it. Now I shall go to feed on the forest and you must protect me.'

The noise of the fire crackling and burning could be heard from miles around. Not a living thing escaped the fury of Arjuna and Krishna's attack. There was consternation in the heavens. Indra was furious that Arjuna, his son, was defying him and taking sides with Agni. He decided to defend the forest.

The sky grew dark as night as Indra's favourite rainclouds, Pushkala and Avartaka, gathered above the forest. Arjuna took the Gandiva and shot up a never-ending blanket of arrows, so that not a drop of rain could reach the forest. He struck down Indra's thunderbolts and banished the rainclouds. But the weight of the rainwater broke through the blanket of arrows and descended in sheets. The fire hissed and wavered from the

onslaught of water. Arjuna quickly sped a fire-mouthed arrow from the Gandiva, which cut through the rain. The sun shone once more and the fire roared again.

The gods of heaven gathered to defend the forest: Varuna, lord of the oceans, seated on a gasping fish, Yama, the god of death, astride a buffalo, Skanda, the god of war, perched on a peacock, his six faces all staring unwaveringly at Arjuna. Even Surya, the sun god, arrived to fight his friend Agni, as did the twin Ashwins, holding green poisonous plants in their hands.

Takshaka, the king of the serpents who ruled the Khandava forest, was away at the time, but his son Avasena was caught in the fire. The serpent queen, Avasena's mother, came to his defence, battling the might of Arjuna's weapons and the venom and fury of the devouring fire. She rose in the sky, hissing with anger, and Arjuna killed her with three sharp arrows. As she died, she saw Avasena slither off to safety and she was content that she had done her duty.

Indra was secretly pleased with this display of Arjuna's prowess at war. He descended to earth and approached the duo, gently requesting his son to desist from more fighting. 'You can ask me for a boon,' he smiled, upon which Arjuna begged him excitedly for his store of divine weapons or astras.

'The time is not ripe,' Indra replied. 'When Sankara, the Lord Shiva, decides to gift you his divine weapon, the Pasupata, then I too shall grant you all my astras.'

As they spoke, an asura called Maya, who was trapped in the fire, came rushing out of the crackling flames. Even as he fell at Arjuna's feet, Krishna raised his hand to destroy him with his Chakra. But Arjuna restrained his friend and saved the asura's life.

The fury of the fire had spent itself. Everything in sight lay destroyed. Agni was satiated and satisfied. Arjuna and Krishna walked to the riverbank, where a cool breeze played on the waters of the Yamuna. The asura Maya followed them, his heart heavy with gratitude. 'You have saved my life,' he said to Arjuna, 'and I too shall do whatever I can for you.'

THE PALACE OF MAYA

Maya was a brilliant architect. He wanted to thank Arjuna by designing the most beautiful palace in the world for the Pandavas' new capital of Indraprastha. He got busy with the plans and designs. In fourteen months, a magnificent building rose from the soil of the once ruined city. It had a thousand columns of gold. The white marble shone like moonbeams at midnight. The windows were netted with gold lattice work, and lamps of shining gems shone in the hallways. Lotus, jasmine and kadamba flowers bloomed in and out of season.

Prayers and ritual havans were conducted before the Pandavas moved into their new palace, which was named Mayasabha. Great feasts were held in the city, and princes and kings arrived from neighbouring kingdoms to join in the celebrations.

Only the Kauravas did not come, although they were of course duly invited. In Hastinapura, Duryodhana and his brothers heard stories of the wonders of Indraprastha and the Mayasabha. They burned with scarcely concealed jealousy and rage at the good fortune of their hated cousins.

Draupadi now had five sons, one by each of the Pandavas. Yudhishthira's son was named Prativindhya, Bhima's Sutasoma, and Arjuna's was called Srutakarman. Nakula's son was named Satanika by Kunti, and Sahadeva's Srutasena. Subhadra, Krishna's sister and Arjuna's new wife, gave birth to a son amidst much rejoicing. She named him Abhimanyu. Abhimanyu was a special favourite of his father. Kunti, who still vividly remembered their days of exile, smiled contentedly, watching her sons prosper. The Pandavas were famous for their glory and righteousness, and princes from kingdoms near and far came to learn the arts of war and statecraft from them.

THE RAJASUYA YAGNA

The sage Narada too came to visit Indraprastha. He examined the wonders of the Mayasabha and declared that the Pandavas' palace was more beautiful than any he had ever seen, grander even than any of the celestial abodes of the gods that he had visited on his travels. 'As the eldest brother, it is your duty to establish your position by performing the Rajasuya yagna,' said Narada to Yudhishthira.

The idea appealed to Yudhishthira. 'How is this Rajasuya yagna to be performed?' he inquired.

'You must send out your emissaries to all corners of Bharatvarsha to declare that you alone are the king of kings. If anyone opposes you or your emissaries, he must be defeated in battle,' Narada explained. 'Next, you must perform the Rajasuya here in Indraprastha, and all your friends and allies must attend. It is not easy to perform such a yagna: if there is anyone who can fulfil this difficult task, it is you, Yudhishthira.'

After Narada left, Yudhishthira consulted with his brothers and Krishna. Krishna was thoughtful. 'There is one king who will be difficult to defeat,' he said. 'King Jarasandha, who rules in Girivraja. My evil uncle Kamsa was married to Jarasandha's daughters. He has never forgiven me, my brother Balarama and our entire Vrishni clan for killing Kamsa. We have met in battle eighteen times. I have defied Jarasandha but never defeated him. It was because of Jarasandha that we had to flee from Mathura to Dwarka.'

Yudhishthira listened carefully to what Krishna had to say. 'I am a peace-loving man,' he said at last. 'There is no reason for me to fight with all the world! Let us forget about the Rajasuya yagna. We are happy and content as we are.'

Bhima was impatient with this attitude. 'Strength, and strength alone, is what matters!' he exclaimed. 'That's what you never seem to understand, my dear brother, with all your talk of peace.'

'No, Bhima, it is not quite so easy,' Krishna warned. 'Jarasandha is a devotee of Lord Shiva and has his protection. He has captured countless kings and holds them captive so that he can offer them as human sacrifices.'

'Why should we be afraid, Yudhishthira?' Arjuna asked, his face glowing with conviction. 'We are all warriors, and you, especially, are the son of Dharma, the god of righteousness. It is our duty to save those kings.'

A little reluctantly, Yudhishthira came around to their point of view. 'Before we begin the Rajasuya, we must defeat Jarasandha,' he said. 'Tell me all about him, Krishna—I am eager to listen to his story.'

And so Lord Krishna told the Pandavas about the strange circumstances of Jarasandha's birth. 'There was once a powerful king named Brihadratha who ruled the kingdom of Magadha,' he said. 'He had two wives, both of whom he loved dearly. They had no children, and this caused Brihadratha much grief. He left his kingdom and went to the forest to meditate. He was accompanied by his two wives, who were twin sisters. There in the forest, he met a famous sage, who was so pleased with his devotion that he gave Brihadratha a magical mango with the blessing that, when his wife ate it, she would bear him a son. The king was a fair and just man. He cut the fruit into two equal halves and gave a piece each to both his beloved queens. His joy when they became pregnant turned to horror when the babies were born. Each queen had given birth to half a child, with one eye, one arm, one leg and so on. The entire palace was repulsed by these monstrosities. At night, when the queens were asleep, the midwife wrapped up the two half-children in black cloth and threw them outside the city gates. That night, a hungry rakshasi named Jara was looking for food. Now rakshasas and rakshasis, like all from the demon world, love the taste of human flesh, and so Jara was delighted to find the two juicy half-children. She held them in her hands, side by side, smacking her lips in anticipation. When the half-children came together, they joined up magically, eye to eye, arm to arm, leg to leg, until the astonished Jara held a beautiful healthy baby in her hands!

'We tend to forget that rakshasas and demons are sometimes the kindest of people. Jara did not have the heart to kill the baby. She felt almost as though she had given birth to it. With her inner vision she knew that this was the child of the king of Magadha. She took the baby to King Brihadratha and told him the story of how the abandoned half-children had become one in her arms.

'The king was delighted and decided to name his son Jarasandha, which means "one who has been joined by Jara".'

Lord Krishna paused. 'That's the story,' he said. 'This is the Jarasandha we have to somehow defeat in battle.'

Yudhishthira was having second thoughts about both the Rajasuya yagna, and unnecessary confrontation with Jarasandha. But his brothers, especially Bhima and Arjuna, were as ever raring for war.

'We cannot defeat Jarasandha in battle,' Krishna said, 'but Bhima is strong enough to defeat him in single combat. The three of us will go to Magadha to defeat Jarasandha, if only you allow us to.'

Reluctantly, Yudhishthira gave his consent, and Krishna, Arjuna and Bhima departed for Girivraja in the kingdom of Magadha.

THE DEATH OF JARASANDHA

Arjuna, Bhima and Krishna reached Magadha after crossing the Sarayu river, travelling through Mithila and then crossing the Ganga river. Before they reached Jarasandha's capital, they dressed themselves as snataks, Brahmin students who have just finished their education. The people of the city noticed them and whispered to each other, wondering who they were.

The disguised Pandavas and Krishna entered Jarasandha's palace not through the main gate, but by nimbly jumping up the walls. Once in the palace, they demanded to meet the king. Jarasandha was deep in his prayers but instructed his staff to feed the guests milk and honey, and request them to wait. They refused the refreshments and waited impatiently. Jarasandha was a devoted worshipper of Lord Shiva and it was well past midnight when at last he finished his prayers.

Jarasandha looked suspiciously at the three men. They looked like warriors, he thought, not snataks. 'You jumped the walls to enter my palace grounds!' he exclaimed. 'You refused my hospitality. Your bodies are not soft like those of students and priests! Your shoulders are scarred with the weight of bows—you are men of arms. Please tell me who you are.'

'We are indeed your enemies,' replied Krishna. 'Warriors are known for their actions, not sweet words. We have come to kill you!'

Jarasandha was puzzled. 'I do not know you,' he replied. 'What wrong have I done you?'

'You have imprisoned helpless kings and kept them captive to sacrifice them to Shiva,' Krishna replied. 'I am Krishna and these are the Pandava brothers Arjuna and Bhima. We have come to challenge you. You can fight whichever of us you please.'

Jarasandha looked at him with contempt. 'So you are the famous Krishna,' he sneered. 'I've defeated you eighteen times already—I wouldn't deign to fight with you again. Arjuna still looks like a little boy! Only Bhima seems big and strong enough to take me on—he's the one I'll fight.'

Jarasandha was not only a brave wrestler but also a dedicated ruler. Although he was quite sure that he would defeat Bhima, he decided to crown his son Sahadeva king so that the kingdom would be safe even if something were to happen to him.

The two opponents, Bhima and Jarasandha, sized each other up before the fight began. Both giants were equally matched in brawn and muscle. Bhima leapt at Jarasandha, who flung him off with ease. They continued their combat relentlessly, not caring if it were day or night. Krishna and Arjuna watched intently, as did a frightened band of courtiers.

Bhima and Jarasandha fought tooth and nail for fourteen days and nights. Gradually Bhima, who was the younger of the two, began to gain the upper hand. As Jarasandha

began to tire, his wily opponent threw him in the air, whirled him around a hundred times and dashed him back to the ground. Then Bhima caught hold of him again and pulled fiercely at his legs, until he had completely ripped Jarasandha apart. Krishna and Arjuna looked on in amazement as the king lay split into two from the middle. Their amazement was only compounded when the two halves seemed to be magically pulled back towards each other, and blood and skin and muscle fused back into a single living breathing whole! The courtiers' tears turned to joy to see their invincible king recover in this miraculous fashion.

Krishna plucked a leaf from a nearby tree. Gaining Bhima's attention, he tore the leaf into two and flung the pieces in opposite directions. Bhima understood immediately what Krishna was telling him. Summoning all the strength at his command, he fell at Jarasandha once more. He took the mighty king in his arms and flung him high into the air. As Jarasandha tumbled down to earth, Bhima took hold of his legs and tore him apart. Then he flung the two halves of Jarasandha's dismembered body as far apart from each other as he possibly could. The two halves flailed about vainly for a while before collapsing. The great king Jarasandha, strongest of the strong, was dead.

While his courtiers and subjects wept, the kings whom Jarasandha had imprisoned were overjoyed at being released. They thanked Krishna and the Pandavas for saving their lives, and promised to come to Indraprastha to attend the Rajasuya yagna in Yudhishthira's honour.

The Pandavas and Krishna went to meet the new king of Magadha, Jarasandha's son Sahadeva, to pay their respects. Krishna took Sahadeva's right hand in his. 'As a son, you must hate me for killing your father,' he said. 'You should understand that I did it because justice had to be done. You must now rule the kingdom of Magadha with honour and courage. If you feel it appropriate, please come to the Rajasuya yagna in our capital.'

Sahadeva was moved by Krishna's humility and promised to visit Indraprastha.

AT THE YAGNA

After their return, the Pandava brothers were sent off in different directions. Arjuna was dispatched to the north, Bhima to the east, Nakula to the western countries and Sahadeva to the south of Bharatvarsha. Everywhere they went they were honoured as emissaries of Yudhishthira. Wherever they found resistance in battle, they defeated their opponents easily with their undisputed excellence in arms.

At last, the day of the Rajasuya dawned. There was an air of festivity and rejoicing throughout Indraprastha. Yudhishthira was formally crowned as the king of kings, the Rajasuya. After the coronation was over, the guests had to be honoured in order of their importance.

Yudhishthira was in a quandary. Who should he honour first? He looked around at the assembly of kings, bewildered by the greatness and grandeur of his guests. There was Drupad, Draupadi's father. Beside him was seated the aged king Vasudeva, father of Krishna and Balarama. There were other rulers of mighty kingdoms from the length and breadth of Bharatvarsha. There was the revered Dronacharya, and their respected teacher Kripa with his son Ashwathama. Perplexed, Yudhishthira asked his grand-uncle Bhishma who it was he should honour first.

The patriarch considered Yudhishthira's question with care. His eyes turned to the radiant figure of Lord Krishna. 'There is your most honoured guest,' he said. 'Krishna has guided you on the path to success and glory. It is to him that you must first pay your respects.'

Sahadeva, the youngest of the Pandavas, came forward to wash Krishna's feet with milk and rose water. The Pandavas' hearts swelled with joy and pride, while Queen Kunti and Draupadi and Subhadra watched approvingly.

But life is never simple. Some of the kings in the assembly did not approve of Bhishma's choice of the guest of honour. Sisupala, king of Chedi, was especially annoyed. He rose to his feet and angrily protested at the respect being shown to Krishna. 'Who is this Krishna?' he spat. 'There are surely many greater kings present here than this lowly cowherd from Mathura! I will not accept this insult to the rest of us. Before this assembly of nobles, I challenge Krishna to a duel.'

Bhima was outraged at Sisupala's audacity, and was about to silence him with a blow, but Bhishma restrained him. 'Do not be in such a hurry, Bhima,' Bhishma counselled. 'It has already been ordained by the gods that Sisupala shall meet his death at Krishna's hands alone. The ways of fate are strange and mysterious, and the mightiest of us must succumb to them!'

And so the assembly of kings, which just some moments ago had been full of joy and rejoicing, grew loud with the clang of weapons and the shouting of angry words.

It had long been predicted by soothsayers and holy men that Sisupala would meet his death at Lord Krishna's hands. Sisupala's mother was the sister of King Vasudeva, Krishna's father. When, many years ago, she first heard of the prophecy, she begged her nephew Krishna to spare her son's life.

'I will try my best not to hurt him,' Krishna had replied. 'I will forgive your son a hundred insults, if need be, rather than get drawn into battle with him.' By now the hundred insults he had promised to overlook had long been exhausted. As a warrior, Krishna had no option save to accept Sisupala's public challenge.

The battle between Krishna and Sisupala began in earnest. The kings and nobles watched uneasily. They were all stunned by this turn of events. The immortals, however, were not surprised. Narada, Bhishma and Vyasa had from the beginning carried a premonition of the turn of events to come. As prophesied, Sisupala died at Krishna's hands.

Yudhishthira, at heart a peace-loving man, was deeply disturbed by what had happened. Somehow, the day wound to a close. The kings left, among mutterings of anger and discontent. Krishna too returned to Dwarka.

All the guests had departed except Duryodhana and Dusasana, their uncle Sakuni, and Karna. The Kauravas and their friends had stayed on to witness first-hand the fabled splendours of the Pandavas' palace, the Mayasabha.

DURYODHANA VISITS THE MAYASABHA

Yudhishthira was glad his cousins had decided to stay on. He and the other Pandavas did their best to see to their guests' comfort. But the Kauravas were consumed by hate and jealousy, and there was very little the Pandavas could do about that.

The asura Maya had built a wondrous and magical palace, where nothing was quite as it appeared to be. What seemed to be a shimmering lake could turn out to be a cunningly designed sheet of marble. A colonnaded doorway would on closer examination reveal itself as a painted mural. These illusions had been created to please and amuse the royal family. Duryodhana had heard of this and was determined not to be taken in.

When Duryodhana entered the main hall, he saw what looked like a shallow indoor pool. Upon closer examination, he decided it was actually an expanse of highly polished marble. He smiled and walked confidently across the hall, only to slip and fall with a splash. He was wet all over, and his fine garments were completely drenched. Only then did he realize that it was in fact a marble pool filled with clear, cool water. His cousins and many of the courtiers turned their faces away to hide their amused smiles; all except Draupadi. The haughty queen of the Pandavas laughed disdainfully at his discomfiture, as Yudhishthira rushed to get him into dry clothes. Proud Duryodhana was angered and humiliated beyond belief. Even as he smiled and tried to look unconcerned, Draupadi's mocking laughter echoed in his ears.

It is sometimes easier to forgive the big things rather than the small ones. After he returned to Hastinapura, Duryodhana swore to avenge the humiliation heaped upon him and to revenge himself on the Pandavas, especially Draupadi.

His cunning and manipulative uncle Sakuni was ready with a plan. 'We will defeat your cousins without battle,' he whispered. 'Bloodshed is not always necessary for victory. That silly Yudhishthira fancies himself as a great gambler. He loves to play games of chance, though he is invariably the loser. We shall invite him to a game of chance, and I shall see that he loses everything—his wealth, his kingdom and even his wife, that arrogant Draupadi.'

Sakuni's idea appealed enormously to Duryodhana. He consulted with his father, the blind king Dhritarashtra, and persuaded him to agree to the plan. Dhritarashtra instructed his architects to build a beautiful hall, to rival the palace built by the Pandavas. Then he requested Vidura to go to Indraprastha to invite the unsuspecting Yudhishthira to come and spend some time with him in Hastinapura.

The Pandavas and Kunti were all highly suspicious of the invitation. 'Nothing is ever as it seems with these Kauravas,' Kunti exclaimed. 'Why has Dhritarashtra invited Yudhishthira to his kingdom?'

'They want to spend time with him, gambling and

playing dice,' Vidura volunteered. 'I personally disapprove of gambling and any games of chance. If I were Yudhishthira, I would be very cautious in accepting this invitation. Yet the king has commanded him to come.'

Yudhishthira was too noble and well brought up to openly refuse his father's brother. 'I must go,' he sighed. 'I will accompany you, Uncle, to that hated city of Hastinapura. And you shall all come with me.'

And so Kunti, Draupadi and the four Pandavas accompanied Vidura and Yudhishthira back to their cousin's capital.

THE GAME OF DICE

The Pandavas arrived in Hastinapura on the night of the full moon. They left their mother and Draupadi in the palace quarters of the Kuru women, and went to the assembly rooms of the new palace, the Jayantasabha.

Karna was there already, as were Bhishma, Dronacharya, Vidura and all the Kaurava brothers. The square dice-cloth was laid out on the marble floor, and by it Sakuni and Duryodhana reclined on embroidered silk cushions. Sakuni's blue eyes glimmered with strange excitement and a malicious smile played about his lips.

'Come, cousin, let us play a game of dice,' Duryodhana said jovially. 'Let us see if fortune favours you or me in a game of chance.'

Sakuni began rolling the dice. 'The highest number wins,' he said, kissing the ivory dice as he spoke. 'I will play for my nephew, staking his wealth against yours.'

'I shall stake all the pearls in my treasury,' Yudhishthira announced.

'I stake the same,' Sakuni responded, shaking the dice deftly before he threw them on the dice-cloth. A sly smile of satisfaction arrived across his thin lips. 'I have won.'

'All the gold in my treasury,' said Yudhishthira, hoping to lure the goddess of good luck with his large-heartedness.

The dice rolled.

'I have won again!' exclaimed Sakuni.

Once again the dice were rolled, this time for all the gems in the coffers at Indraprastha. 'I have won again,' Sakuni exulted.

Yudhishthira knew that he was on a losing streak, but he was too caught up in the excitement of the game to stop. The sounds of Sakuni's voice declaring 'I have won' became a monotonous refrain that kept echoing through the magnificent chamber. Yudhishthira lost his chariots, his horses, his elephants, his army, his granary and even his slaves. Finally, there was nothing left to lose.

'What will you stake now, King Yudhishthira?' Sakuni mocked.

As Sakuni kept goading him on and on, Yudhishthira became more and more reckless.

The fever of gambling had entered Yudhishthira's blood, making him impervious to reason or good sense. 'I stake my handsome brother Nakula,' he said.

'I have won,' declared Sakuni.

'My brother Sahadeva!'

'I win again.'

Yudhishthira was wrestling with his conscience. He knew he was doing the wrong thing, and yet he could not stop.

Sakuni sensed his indecision. 'You are quick to stake your step-brothers, the sons of Madri,' he said scornfully. 'Why do you hesitate when it comes to your blood brothers?'

'Arjuna is my greatest wealth, and I stake him!' exclaimed Yudhishthira.

'I win again,' said Sakuni, kissing the dice in gratitude.

'I wager Bhima!'

'I have won him,' exulted Sakuni.

'I stake myself against my four brothers,' cried Yudhishthira.

'I have won again,' said Sakuni. 'What now?'

'I must stake my wife Draupadi,' said Yudhishthira, a note of utter desperation in his voice.

'I win again! Draupadi belongs to the Kauravas!'

There was dead silence in the hall. Everyone was horror-struck. No one knew what might happen next. Only Dhritarashtra could be heard, muttering excitedly, 'Who has won the wager? Is it my Duryodhana?'

Duryodhana turned triumphantly to Vidura. 'Draupadi is now our slave!' he declared. 'Pray bring her to the assembly to stand before us.'

'I will not do as you say,' replied Vidura. 'Yudhishthira had no right to stake her when he had already lost himself in the wager!'

Nonetheless, a servant was sent to the women's quarters to summon Draupadi. 'Your husband Yudhishthira has gambled you away to the Kauravas,' the servant told her, a look of pity and compassion in his eyes.

'Has he lost his senses? How can he gamble me away?' Draupadi asked.

'It is so,' said the servant. 'First he lost all his treasure, then his brothers, then himself, until finally he lost you at the game of dice.'

Tired of waiting, Dusasana came storming in to take Draupadi back to the chamber by force. He grabbed her by her long black hair and pulled and dragged her behind him to the gathered assembly.

Draupadi was a proud woman. She could not be humbled so easily. Her eyes flashed fire as she shook loose her hair and angrily accosted the gathered men. 'Honoured elders,' she said, 'I just want to ask one question. If my husband had already lost himself, how then could he stake me in the game of dice?' She looked around her, trying to keep calm, to appeal to the better instincts of the roomful of men. 'Am I a slave of my husband, or am I free? Tell me this, grandfather Bhishma, wisest of the wise.'

Bhishma shifted uncomfortably in his chair, more than a little disturbed by Draupadi's question. In his eyes, women were the possessions of their menfolk, to be protected by their fathers, husbands and sons. 'Although a man cannot gamble something that does not belong to him, yet a man maintains a right over his wife,' he said finally. 'He can call her his property even after he has lost himself.'

Not all the Kaurava brothers were as evil and hard-hearted as Duryodhana or Dusasana. One of the younger Kauravas, Vikarna, was deeply moved by Draupadi's plight. He stood up to speak in her defence. 'I protest,' he said. 'Yudhishthira had no right to stake Draupadi and gamble her away, for she is married not only to him but to his brothers as well. He did not seek the consent of the other Pandavas before wagering her.'

The entire assembly was silenced by Vikarna's fair-minded and logical observation. But Dusasana was getting impatient of all the arguments. He grabbed hold of the end of Draupadi's sari and began pulling at it, with the intention of disrobing her and leaving her naked in the assembly hall.

Draupadi looked around her, horrified, but no one came to her aid. No one would meet her eyes. She could not believe that this injustice was being done to her. 'I shall pray to Krishna,' she resolved. 'He is the protector of the weak, and the last refuge of the helpless. Save me, Krishna, wherever you are!'

Krishna, though he was not there in the Kauravas' palace, heard Draupadi's prayer. As the Pandava queen stood before the assembly, her eyes shut and her palms folded in prayer, the length of her silken garments magically grew and grew and grew. The more the astonished Dusasana tugged and pulled, the greater the length of multi-hued silken cloth that heaped up in a mountain of colour before him.

Everyone in the hall—the Pandavas, the Kauravas and the assembled courtiers—knew that they were witnessing a miracle. The gods and immortals were clearly siding with Draupadi, who had been so cruelly wronged by Duryodhana and his brother. The evil Dusasana finally fell to the ground in an exhausted heap, surrounded by miles and miles of shimmering silk.

Bhima could no longer control himself. The strange situation had forced him, the strongest man in the world, to watch helplessly as his

beloved Draupadi was insulted in public. His loud voice rang through the hall, echoing with determination and the shadow of future deaths. 'Hear me,' he announced. 'I declare today that I shall kill the proud Duryodhana, as my brother Arjuna shall kill Karna. As for Sakuni, he shall be killed by Sahadeva. After I have killed Duryodhana with my mace, I shall place my foot on his bleeding head. And then I shall drink the blood from the heart of this cowardly Dusasana, who attacks the women whom he, as a Kuru, should be protecting.'

Arjuna walked to the centre of the hall. 'No one has ever escaped the wrath of Bhima,' he said. 'The earth shall drink the blood of these four: Duryodhana, Dusasana, Sakuni and Karna. I will kill everyone who is foolish enough to support them.'

Now it was the turn of Sahadeva. 'Remember Sakuni, with the dice you rolled today and gloated over, you have strung the bow of the swift, sure arrows that spell out your death. I shall destroy you and all your kinsmen,' he vowed.

Nakula came forward. 'I stand by all that my brothers said,' he declared. 'I shall kill Uluka, the son of Sakuni, and ensure that his line is destroyed forever.'

Yudhishthira, who had been standing alone, still and silent through all the tumult, took Arjuna's hand in his and drew him aside. He was a peace-loving man and he looked thoughtful and pained by all the anger around him. 'I too wanted to kill them all,' he said, sorrowfully, 'until I happened to see Karna's feet. They are so like the feet of our mother Kunti that all my anger ebbed away.'

Little did he realize then that Karna was his brother, born of Kunti. But that is the way with war and anger and revenge; we never know who we are destroying and why.

Old King Dhritarashtra's excitement began to turn into anxiety. He sensed that his sons had overstepped all the limits of caution. His heart trembled as he heard the death-vows of the Pandavas. He tried now to pacify Draupadi. 'Please forgive my sons for their behaviour,' he pleaded. 'I will grant you any boon you wish.'

'Release my husband Yudhishthira from bondage,' she replied, a plea to which Dhritarashtra immediately agreed.

'You may have another boon, daughter Draupadi,' he said placatingly.

This time the Pandava queen requested that the other four brothers be released as well. Dhritarashtra agreed immediately, and granted her another boon.

Draupadi turned away proudly. 'My husbands are free. I ask for nothing else,' she replied.

Karna took the opportunity to give vent to his hatred. 'You are mighty warriors indeed, O Pandavas!' he sneered. 'You have been saved by a woman!'

Their hearts saddened by pain and humiliation, the Pandavas prepared to return to Indraprastha.

THE SECOND EXILE

Dusasana rushed to Duryodhana and Sakuni, who had returned to their chambers. 'Our plans have been overturned,' he lamented. 'Father has restored everything to the Pandavas!'

Duryodhana confronted his father. 'Let us play just one more game,' he pleaded. 'Whoever wins will rule the kingdom. The loser and his kin shall be exiled to the forest for twelve years. They must spend the thirteenth year in disguise. If, during the thirteenth year, their identity is revealed, they shall have to spend another twelve years in the forest.'

Dhritarashtra was a weak man. He wavered once more and then agreed. He sent a messenger to call the Pandavas back. 'The king, your uncle, requests you to return to Hastinapura,' the messenger said. 'He wants you to play just one more game of dice.'

Yudhishthira was noble and honourable to a fault. Although he already knew what the outcome of the game would be, he decided to return to Hastinapura. 'I must honour my uncle's wish,' he sighed. 'I shall play again.'

The Pandavas returned once more to the grand hall in the Jayantasabha. Queen Kunti and Draupadi waited outside, for they did not want to go to the women's quarters.

Sakuni stipulated the conditions of the game. 'All our fortunes rest on this one throw of the dice,' he said. 'The loser will have to spend twelve years in the forest, and the year thirteenth in disguise. If this disguise is uncovered, the losers, whomsoever they might be, shall be exiled for another twelve years.'

The other Pandavas tried to dissuade Yudhishthira from playing, but he was a gambler at heart. He could not resist the thrill of the dice. 'Perhaps I shall win this time,' he told himself.

Yudhishthira sat quietly before Sakuni, and watched the dice roll as they decided his fate.

'I have won,' declared Sakuni, as Yudhishthira had in his heart of hearts known he would.

The Pandavas prepared to go into exile. They dressed themselves in garments made of bark and deerskin, for they were no longer kings now but hermits and wanderers.

Duryodhana's heart was heavy with mixed and confused feelings. He knew he had done wrong, but his envy of the Pandavas was so deep and destructive that he no longer cared. He turned to Dhritarashtra, who was lamenting quietly. Yet the blind king's firstborn son was still his greatest weakness, and he could refuse him nothing.

Duryodhana sensed his father's feelings. 'I am what I am,' he said. 'I must follow the compulsions of my nature. Remember, Father, that peaceful kings are always destroyed. Only discontent can lead to happiness.'

Vidura pleaded with his nephews to leave Kunti with him, and they agreed. 'Take care of your brothers, Yudhishthira,' Kunti said bravely as they parted. 'I shall not be with you in the forest this time, but my thoughts will never leave you.'

Vidura blessed them tenderly as they departed. 'May the moon give you patience and the earth give you strength,' he said. 'Do not forget all that you have learnt from your earlier wanderings.'

Arjuna sent a messenger to Indraprastha requesting his other wife Subhadra to return to her family in Dwarka. The Pandavas and Draupadi left Hastinapura through the south gate, the gate of death.

THE DEPARTURE

Dhritarashtra was alone in his chamber. He sent for Vidura. 'Have the Pandavas left?' he asked, his face masked to hide his true feelings. 'Tell me of their departure.'

'Draupadi went first,' sighed Vidura, 'her beautiful face covered by her long perfumed hair. She was weeping as though she would never stop. She was followed by Yudhishthira, his face covered up with a cloth, so that his righteous anger might not burn up Hastinapura with a look. He was followed by Bhima, who was flexing and unflexing the muscles of his mighty hands, his mind set only on revenge. Behind him was Arjuna, radiant even in exile, who was casting grains of sand in all directions as he left.'

'Why was he doing that?' Dhritarashtra inquired.

'Because he has sworn revenge,' Vidura replied. 'Each grain of sand represents one of the million arrows with which he will destroy Hastinapura.'

Narada, the messenger of the gods, appeared before Dhritarashtra and Vidura. 'You have committed a grave injustice,' he declared. 'In fourteen years, all the Kauravas will be destroyed. You and your sons will reap the fruits of your injustice. Enjoy your kingdom while you can, for this illusion of power and victory will not last for long. Death stalks your family, Dhritarashtra.'

As the Pandavas left Hastinapura, their family priest Dhaumya accompanied them. He plucked some kusa grass from the south gate and then he recited some verses from the holy Sama Veda, addressed to Rudra and Yama, the gods of retribution and death. 'These are the funeral prayers for the sons of King Dhritarashtra,' he announced. 'One day the whole city will resound with these lamentations.'

The Pandavas walked fast, for they wanted to get away from Hastinapura as soon as they could. They arrived at the banks of the Ganga, where they drank the sweet pure

water and slept in the shade of trees. Now that they were wanderers in the forest, they had to hunt for food, or live on fruits, nuts and roots.

Dhaumya suggested that Yudhishthira pray to the sun for help, for the sun is the source of light and energy, and feeds and sustains the world. Yudhishthira prayed with deep concentration.

The sun god Surya appeared before him and gifted him a copper vessel. 'You will never lack for food,' he declared. 'As soon as Draupadi puts a spoon into this copper bowl, she will get all the food she needs.'

The brothers decided to halt for a while in the forest of Kamyaka. Krishna, accompanied by Draupadi's brother Dhrishtadyumya and some other kings, went to visit them there. 'Let us go to war against the Kauravas,' Krishna suggested. 'We can easily defeat them in battle. A day of the gods is equal to a mortal year. After twelve days have passed, and a thirteenth has been spent in disguise, you can take revenge on the Kauravas.'

But Yudhishthira was adamant. 'We are not gods but mortals,' he sighed. 'I have given my word. We must suffer our fate.'

Draupadi was both happy and unhappy to see her brother and Krishna. All the grief and humiliation that she was holding within her came pouring out in a torrent of tears. 'Only you came to my aid when Dusasana tried to disrobe me,' she sobbed to Krishna. 'Yudhishthira's patience and restraint are driving me mad! Why can't he get angry, as any normal person would! Too much goodness is an unbearable thing!'

Krishna tried to wipe her tears away. 'Wait a while longer, Draupadi,' he said. 'The

women of the Kauravas will weep as you do now. When Duryodhana lies slaughtered on the battlefield, when Bhima has drunk of Dusasana's blood, and when Karna's body is pockmarked by Arjuna's arrows, then it will be their turn to weep.'

Krishna turned to Yudhishthira. 'We shall see you as king again,' he prophesied. 'I shall crown you with these very hands.' Then Krishna and the other kings returned to their own lands, leaving the Pandavas to ponder over the mysterious workings of fate.

ARJUNA'S TRAVELS

After a while, the Pandavas grew restless in the Kamyaka forest. They decided to travel to Dwaitavana, a dense green forest where peacocks danced and nightingales sang.

The brothers tried their best to be philosophical about their troubles. Only Bhima could not be calmed. His eyes were always red with anger and he spent sleepless nights reliving the scene of Draupadi's humiliation. He would sit alone in the forest, wringing his hands in helpless fury.

Draupadi too could neither forgive nor forget. She would taunt Yudhishthira and mock him for his patience. 'I know you are the son of Dharma, the god of justice and righteousness,' she said. 'But a warrior who controls his anger is no warrior at all! I am tired of your unending patience!'

Yudhishthira had not forgiven himself for the foolish gambling that had led to their ruin. 'I deserve your criticism,' he said, 'and so I am silent before your reproaches. But your angry words cannot make me change my ideas of right and wrong. If, at the end of thirteen years, Duryodhana refuses to return our kingdom to us, then I shall be as angry as you want me to be. I will not then be the same Yudhishthira who stood silent at the court of the Kauravas. Remember, anger is the greatest of all weapons and it must be used with greatest restraint.'

The Pandavas resolved to spend the years of their exile in making themselves stronger in preparation of the war that would inevitably follow. They would have their revenge and they could wait for it.

In the sixth year of their exile, the sage Vyasa visited them in Dwaitavana. 'Yudhishthira, you must send Arjuna on a journey to the north,' he said. 'When Arjuna helped Agni to consume the Khandava forest, his father Indra was well pleased with his valour. He promised to some day give him all his weapons, but only after Lord Shiva had seen fit to gift him with the Pasupata, the greatest weapon of them all. It is time now for Arjuna to pray and do penance to win Shiva's favour. After he has received the gift of Shiva's Pasupata, he can claim Indra's armoury of magical weapons.'

Bhima's eyes were gleaming at the prospect of war and weapons. Arjuna prepared himself immediately to depart for the Himalayas, where he would engage in penances and pray for Shiva's grace. As for the rest, they decided, upon the advice of Vyasa, to move back to the Kamyaka forest from Dwaitavana.

Arjuna walked through endless tracts of dense forest and climbed up the low foothills until he reached the mountains of Gandhamdama, which he had visited earlier, at the time of the Rajasuya yagna. Then he climbed even higher, and crossed the Himavana until he reached the mountain peak of Indrakila.

There Arjuna encountered an old hermit with a white beard and a gentle face. 'Weapons are of no use here, my child,' the hermit said to him. 'This is the abode of monks and holy men who have conquered passion and anger. They need no armour, no bow and arrows, for they have nothing to defend!'

But Arjuna knew what he wanted. He bowed low before the hermit. 'O holy sage, I seek the deadliest arms and the most destructive weapons of war. Bless me in my quest,' he persisted.

The old man was actually Indra in disguise. He now revealed himself to his son Arjuna. 'I shall gift you with my entire arsenal of divine astras, once you have won the favour of Lord Shiva and obtained the Pasupata,' Indra declared.

Arjuna remained lost in prayer for many days. Lord Shiva decided to visit him in the guise of a hunter. He was accompanied by his wife Parvati, who was dressed in the rough garments of a huntress.

As Arjuna prayed, a rakshasa named Mooka assumed the form of a wild boar and charged at him. Arjuna picked up his bow, the Gandiva, and released a volley of arrows. Shiva appeared before him, disguised as a hunter, and protested that the boar was his. Then Shiva too let forth an arrow, which pierced the animal as it lay dying.

A strange, eerie light floated through the mountains. Puzzled, Arjuna tried to find its source. He found that it emanated from the hunter and huntress. 'You have broken the rules of hunting, which dictate that two hunters shall not aim at the same target,' Arjuna chided them. 'I shall have to challenge you.'

The hunter smiled amusedly. 'You are a brave young man, but hot-headed,' he said. 'Do you really dare to challenge me?'

A furious battle ensued. Arjuna enveloped his opponent in a cloak of arrows, but the mysterious hunter removed them with a shrug and a smile. 'It is a pleasure to fight with you,' he said. 'We must continue.'

Arjuna reached for his arrow, to find the inexhaustible quiver suddenly empty. He lashed out with his bow, the Gandiva, but it seemed to have no effect on his opponent. Arjuna reached for his sword, but it wilted in his hands like a lotus stem. He tried to hurl stones at the hunter, but he just stood there, with the huntress behind him, smiling maddeningly.

By now the invincible Arjuna was faint with exhaustion. He closed his eyes and prayed to Lord Shiva to come to his aid. In his mind he offered a garland of flowers to the god. Then, very slowly, he opened his weary eyes again.

He saw the slaughtered boar, which had changed back into the rakshasa Mooka. The hunter stood before him, with the same enigmatic smile on his glowing face. The garland of flowers which Arjuna had offered to Shiva was strung around the hunter's bow.

At last, Arjuna understood that the mysterious hunter was none other than Lord Shiva himself. He fell at his feet and begged pardon for challenging him.

'You are pardoned, my child,' Shiva replied. 'I came in disguise so that I could test your courage and valour. You have proved yourself. You shall have the Pasupata, but on one condition. You must never use it, unless it is absolutely necessary.'

Lord Shiva gifted Arjuna the mighty and invincible Pasupata, the one weapon above all others that he had always coveted. He taught the Pandava all the holy invocations to release and retract it.

'You may go now, Arjuna, to your father's heaven, Indraloka. Tell him that I think you are worthy of the Pasupata,' Shiva declared. Arjuna's heart overflowed with happiness.

AT INDRALOKA

Arjuna was eager to meet his father and get his hands on Indra's magical weapons. As Arjuna prepared to set off for Indraloka, suddenly a radiant white light lit up the peaks and forests of Indrakila, where he had so recently battled with Lord Shiva. The gods and immortals had assembled to bless Arjuna. There was his father, Indra, lord of the heavens, accompanied by Varuna, Yama and Kubera. They smiled fondly at the young Pandava and came forward to bless him.

Yama, the lord of death, master of the south, gave him his invincible weapon, the noose. 'This astra will protect you in the war which you are destined to fight,' Yama said.

Next Varuna, master of the west, lord of the oceans, stepped forward, and gifted him a mace. 'This is the Varunastra, which is my gift to you,' he said. 'Its powers will manifest themselves at the right time, exactly when you need them.'

Next Kubera, lord of wealth, master of the north, gave a special weapon to Arjuna. 'This astra will grant you all the wealth of the earth and the heavens,' he declared. 'After you and your brothers have won the war, you will use it well.'

Arjuna was overcome with gratitude. Although he was the son of Indra, Arjuna himself was a mortal. 'I cannot believe that the gods have been so kind to me!' he exclaimed as he bowed before them in gratitude and humility.

Indra sent his charioteer Matali to carry Arjuna to the heaven of Indraloka. Indra himself, like all the gods, could travel to a place by merely thinking of where he wanted to be. Arjuna, as a mortal, had to take the magical chariot drawn by horses with winged hooves driven by Matali. They flew through several layers of fleecy clouds, passing the source of the holy river, the Ganga. They halted at Mount Mandara to rest the horses and to let them drink from the crystal clear streams that flowed around the mountain. Finally, they arrived at Indra's palace at Amaravati, the city of the immortals.

Amaravati was the most magical place Arjuna had ever seen. There was constant music and dancing day and night. The gods were attended upon by the gandharvas, heavenly beings skilled in music, and apsaras, celestial women of incredible and everlasting beauty. Their youth was eternal and they smelt of lilies and roses. The four celestial apsaras at Indra's court were Menaka, Rambha, Tilottama and Urvashi. They danced and sang and gladdened the hearts of all who saw them.

Indra was delighted that his son Arjuna was at last visiting his palace, especially as Shiva had proclaimed him a great warrior and given him the Pasupata. He seated Arjuna beside him on his royal throne and instructed the apsaras to keep his son suitably entertained.

Urvashi, Indra's favourite apsara, fell hopelessly in love with the dark, handsome young man with the scarred shoulders. She could not eat or sleep, for she spent all her time lost in dreams of Arjuna. Urvashi was an ageless, immortal beauty, who was used to mortals and immortals falling in love with her with no effort on her part. But Arjuna, although he was unfailingly polite, showed no signs whatsoever of succumbing to her charms. She tried to entice him with inviting looks, she dressed herself in glittering garments and wore garlands of fragrant flowers, she danced with all the grace and rhythm she was famous for. But try as she would, Urvashi could not get Arjuna to fall in love with her.

'I love you, Arjuna,' she burst out at last. 'I want to spend all my life with you.'

Arjuna was alarmed. His goal in visiting Indra's palace was to get his father's magical weapons. His mind was set only upon the war the Pandavas had resolved to fight, to avenge Draupadi's humiliation and win back their kingdom from the Kauravas. He had neither the time nor the desire to fall in love. He was already married to Draupadi and to Subhadra, Lord Krishna's sister. He had two sons, Srutakarman and Abhimanyu. There was no place in his life for Urvashi and her simpering looks.

'I pledge you my love, Arjuna,' Urvashi said soulfully, 'and seek yours in return.'

'But you are much older than me,' Arjuna stuttered tactlessly. 'You are like my mother Kunti!'

Urvashi was well and truly offended. Her vanity was hurt and she suddenly became very vicious indeed. 'I am an immortal, a celestial being,' she retorted. 'Apsaras have no age, for we grow no older with the passage of time. Those things happen only to you mortals!'

'I am sorry, Urvashi, but I cannot love you,' Arjuna said apologetically.

The lovely apsara's fine eyes flashed with fire. 'I shall avenge this insult,' she shrieked. 'I curse you! Although you rejected my love, you will not be able to reject this curse! You are so proud, O Arjuna, of being a brave and manly warrior, but you will become a eunuch and spend your days surrounded by women, dancing for their amusement.'

Arjuna was devastated by Urvashi's curse. He rushed to his father for advice.

'No one has ever been able to resist Urvashi's beauty,' Indra exclaimed. 'A curse cannot be withdrawn, but I can certainly persuade her to reduce it to just one year. Perhaps, in future, in the thirteenth year of your exile, Urvashi's curse might help you find a suitable disguise to hide from the Kauravas.'

Arjuna was somewhat relieved by the answer. Indra requested Urvashi to forgive his son and reconsider the curse. She agreed, and although she was still angered by the handsome mortal's refusal, she assured to limit the curse to a year.

Arjuna spent the rest of his time in Amaravati learning the arts of dance and music from the gandharva king Chitrasena. Chitrasena's lessons were to be infinitely useful when, in the thirteenth year of his exile, Arjuna had to live out Urvashi's curse.

Every day in heaven is a year on earth. The six earthly years Arjuna spent in Indra's palace passed in just so many days. Indra taught Arjuna the precise use of his divine astras, and then, when it was time for him to leave, sadly bade him farewell.

Meanwhile, the other brothers were missing Arjuna dreadfully. He was the most cheerful and charming of the Pandavas, and life was very dull without him. Bhima would constantly quarrel with Yudhishthira, criticizing him for being too tolerant and patient, while Draupadi would weep at the fate that had overtaken them all.

The great sage Brihadaswa came to visit the Pandavas in the forest. Yudhishthira, who was full of grief and self-reproach, burst into tears before the holy man. 'Have you ever seen or heard of anyone more unfortunate than me?' he sobbed.

Brihadaswa consoled Yudhishthira by telling him the story of Nala, the Nishadha king who too had lost his kingdom in a game of dice. Nala had suffered great misery and hardship, as had his wife Damyanti, until he learnt the secret art of winning at dice. This art was known as the Akshahridiya. 'I shall teach you this secret art, Yudhishthira,' the sage promised. He took him away for three days, and taught the son of Dharma how to speak to the dice so that they would always obey his command.

Yudhishthira was reassured by Brihadaswa's stories and instruction. If Nala, the king of Nishadha, could reverse his fortunes, why, the Pandavas would be able to do so as well. And now that he had learnt the secrets of the Akshahridiya, Sakuni and Duryodhana would no longer be able to trick him at the dice-board.

The Pandavas decided to go on a long pilgrimage. They went to Mount Kailash, in the high Himalayas, crossing a hundred steep hills before they reached there. The forests were full of flowers and birdsong. It was the first time in the long period of their exile that Draupadi was happy. She would smile with wonder at all the exotic and beautiful blossoms that she saw, and Bhima would rush and pluck whichever flowers she desired.

One morning Draupadi was walking through the sloping woods when the east wind wafted a lovely blossom into her hands. It was a white lotus with a thousand petals. It had an intoxicating fragrance, and a hundred butterflies fluttered in homage around it.

'Oh, how I wish I had another of these flowers,' Draupadi sighed.

Bhima, who always did whatever he could to make Draupadi happy, set off in search of the thousand-petalled lotus. As he rushed across the forest paths he encountered the monkey god Hanuman, who like Bhima, was the son of Vayu, lord of the wind. Hanuman blessed Bhima, and told him that, when the war with the Kauravas began, he would be there to aid the Pandavas.

Bhima continued to walk north, following the heady perfume of the thousand-petalled lotus. Guided by his sense of smell, he arrived at a beautiful meadow, at the centre of which was a still and shimmering lake, abloom with hundreds of white lotus flowers. This was the garden of Kubera, the god of wealth, but Bhima did not know this.

As Bhima began plucking the flowers from the lake for Draupadi, Kubera's guards tried to stop him. Bhima dealt with them in his usual forcible way. The frightened guards went to complain to their master Kubera about the terrifying trespasser.

'That sounds like Bhima,' laughed Kubera, and went forth to greet his Pandava friend. He wanted to hold a feast in Bhima's honour, but for once the huge warrior declined a good meal.

'I must hurry back to Draupadi,' he exclaimed, 'or these stolen flowers will wilt and my search will have been in vain.'

So the days passed, sometimes cheerfully, sometimes clouded with sadness, and then the months, and gradually the years. When the Pandavas reached the hermitage of Badari, they enjoyed the clear air of the mountain retreat.

One evening, they saw an unearthly light radiating from the mountain slope. Indra's chariot was rushing towards them, carrying Arjuna in it. As Matali brought his vehicle to a halt, Arjuna rushed out to greet his long-lost family. They did not sleep for many nights, as Arjuna regaled them with tales of his adventures and stories of the wonders of Amaravati and Indraloka.

The period of exile was drawing to a close. The Pandavas, especially Draupadi, were sad at leaving the beautiful mountains, which had offered them so much solace and comfort. Their thoughts returned to their cousins, the Kauravas.

'It is time to remember our oaths of vengeance,' Bhima declared. 'Even my dear Yudhishthira must shed his patience after our period of exile is over.'

THE BATTLE WITH THE GANDHARVAS

In the twelfth year of their exile, the Pandavas left the high mountains and returned to Kamyaka forest, near the still waters of the Dwaitavana lake. Their movements came to the notice of the Kaurava brothers, and Duryodhana began burning with the old intense fever of jealousy. He was driven mad by his desire to actually see the Pandavas in exile and witness their discomfort. Goaded by Sakuni and Karna, who hated the Pandavas almost as much as he did, Duryodhana set off for the Dwaitavana lake.

The Kuru warriors set up their tents in the forest. They laughed and drank and feasted. Duryodhana wanted to set up a pleasure house by the lake where he could spend time with his favourite wives and slave-women. His scouts and spies were, meanwhile, instructed to swim to all corners of the lake to discover the whereabouts of the Pandavas.

The Kuru soldiers strutted to the water front. Suddenly they were stopped in their tracks by two smiling gandharvas.

'Move aside,' said the Kuru soldiers, in their rough voices. 'Duryodhana, the foremost of the Kauravas, has come to the Dwaitavana lake with his queens. Go away, there is no place for you here!'

'The Dwaitavana lake is closed by the orders of the gandharva king,' the gandharvas said, gently but firmly.

'Duryodhana is the mightiest of the Kauravas!' the Kuru soldiers barked.

The gandharvas were unruffled. 'The gandharva king is a celestial,' they replied in their musical voices. 'He does not have to give way to a mere mortal.'

The soldiers tried to push the unarmed gandharvas aside, and even drew arms against them, but try as they would, they could not budge them or get past their glowing bodies.

When Duryodhana came to know of this encounter, he gathered his troops and marched towards the Dwaitavana lake. Soon his soldiers were drawn into furious combat with the gandharvas. The gandharvas are normally peace-loving, but they are immortals and it

was impossible for the mortal Kauravas to defeat them in battle. The artistic gandharvas understood the art of creating illusions and would confuse their opponents effortlessly. They would throw flowers that would turn into balls of fire and spread sheets of blinding light above the panicking Kaurava army. Each gandharva would multiply into ten mirror-images of himself. Frightened and bewildered, the Kaurava soldiers ran away, but Karna continued to fight undaunted. Duryodhana's elephant ran trumpeting in fear towards the lake. Finally, Karna, too, had to leap from his chariot and run away. And all this while soft gandharva music played in the heavens, as though mocking the Kauravas' defeat.

Duryodhana, Dusasana, Sakuni and their wives were all captured by the smiling gandharvas. Duryodhana found himself flung into an iron net which was hung from the sky and left suspended there.

His despairing soldiers and courtiers now belatedly found the Pandava camp and rushed there for help. They fell at Yudhishthira's feet and begged him to come to their rescue. 'Duryodhana is captured by the gandharvas!' they exclaimed. 'His wives are held captive by them! You must help us!'

Bhima was delighted by their desperation. 'Duryodhana deserves to be punished,' he gloated. 'Whatever makes you think that we will come to his aid?'

Yudhishthira reproached his brother. 'It is our duty to defend our cousins,' he said quietly. 'They may be our enemies but they are still our blood brothers. We may fight amongst ourselves, but when they are attacked by a third party, we must help them.'

Bhima could not believe his ears. He went red with anger and began flexing and unflexing his muscles in frustration. But Yudhishthira was stern. 'We are five against a hundred,' he said. 'But against a common enemy, we are a hundred and five. Take Arjuna, Nakula and Sahadeva with you, and rescue Duryodhana.'

Bhima remained unconvinced, and so Yudhishthira, the son of the lord of righteousness, tried another line of argument. 'We are destined to fight and destroy the Kauravas,' he explained. 'But for the moment, our duty lies in rescuing them. You must follow my command and go to their aid.'

The Pandavas obeyed Yudhishthira and fell into furious battle with the gandharvas. The brothers were mortals, but they were all sons of gods and immortals. Bhima got busy with his mace, while Arjuna rained a blanket of arrows from his magical bow, the Gandiva. The gandharvas began to tire under the assault.

Suddenly, a peal of musical laughter echoed through the sky. A rainbow appeared and behind it stood Chitrasena, the king of the gandharvas. Arjuna was surprised and delighted to see his friend, who had instructed him in the arts of dance and music. 'Whatever are you doing here, Chitrasena?' he asked.

'Your father, Lord Indra, sent me,' said Chitrasena. 'He came to know of Duryodhana's plans to humiliate you and we thought we would turn the tables upon him. Your dear cousin is at your mercy now! You can do what you please with him.'

'You must let Duryodhana go,' Arjuna replied. 'That is what Yudhishthira desires.'

'Then Yudhishthira must come himself to free him,' said Chitrasena. And so the humiliated Duryodhana was released by the gandharvas and handed over to the oldest of the Pandava brothers.

'You may go, Duryodhana,' Yudhishthira said courteously. 'You are free to return to Hastinapura again. Your wives, your brothers, your troops, all may return with you.'

Duryodhana's humiliation was complete. This was even worse than being captured by the gandharvas. Too petty to thank his cousin for his magnanimity, he proudly turned his face away and left without a word, choked by an anger and helplessness he could not contain.

PLOTTING REVENGE

Duryodhana dispatched his army back to Hastinapura. He stayed on in the forest camp, hurt and humiliated by his defeat at the hands of the gandharva king and Yudhishthira's generosity in releasing him. 'I was forgiven by my enemy,' he lamented, 'and released along with the women. I shall kill myself, I shall starve to death here in this forest. Dusasana must become king in my place.'

Dusasana, Karna and Sakuni had stayed on in the forest to console the despondent Duryodhana. 'The bond between us is as strong as that between those Pandavas,' Dusasana exclaimed. 'I would never accept the crown of Hastinapura in your stead!'

'I have been defeated and pitied! I can't bear to think about it,' the eldest Kaurava moaned.

'I love you as much as your brothers do,' Karna reassured him. 'If you should decide to die, why, I will die with you! And look at it like this—the Pandavas didn't really defeat the gandharvas! Arjuna is a friend of Chitrasena, the gandharva king, and they staged the whole thing between them.'

Sakuni had been watching his nephew with an amused smile. 'What a big baby you are!' he said. 'For all your grand words, you are acting like a spoilt brat. Grief and suffering strengthen character, but perhaps you have been too pampered all along.'

'Look at the Pandavas,' Karna pointed out tactlessly. 'They didn't cry or complain when they were sent into exile.' This statement upset Duryodhana all the more.

Sakuni knew how to handle Duryodhana. 'I have the perfect solution,' he said, a sneer playing on his lips. 'All you have to do to redeem yourself is to restore the kingdom to the noble Pandavas. Everyone will praise your generosity, and the whole episode will be forgotten.'

This wasn't what Duryodhana wanted to hear. 'I shall spend the night in the forest, meditating on what I must do,' he declared. He spread out a mat of kusa grass, closed his eyes in prayer and beseeched the fates to show him what to do next.

A prayer must be pure and come from the heart, only then is it heard and answered. Duryodhana's mind and heart were shrivelled and warped by hatred and envy. Kaalla, the demon of wrong advice and misdirection, who feeds on false pride and mistrust, came and perched himself on Duryodhana's left shoulder. 'You shall rule the earth,' lying Kaalla whispered into his ear. 'Why should you think of giving up the world when it is yours to rule? Karna, Dusasana, Bhishma, Drona and Ashwathama are all there to fight for you, and to die for you if necessary. Do not bow before the Pandavas! Defeat them in battle and be the king of all you survey!'

His words heartened Duryodhana immeasurably. Kaalla had set the eldest of the Kauravas on a course of action that would destroy not only him, but his entire clan.

So Duryodhana returned to Hastinapura, planning revenge against the Pandavas, who had never deliberately done him any harm. Encouraged by Karna, his faithful friend, Duryodhana set out to perform the Rajasuya yagna. All the neighbouring kings were either made to submit to him and pay tribute, or were defeated in battle by the valiant Karna.

The coronation ceremony for the Rajasuya was planned on a grand scale, for Duryodhana was determined to outdo the one the Pandavas had performed at Indraprastha. A special messenger was sent to the forest to invite the exiled Pandavas to the yagna ceremony.

'I would be happy to come,' Yudhishthira said gently, 'but I cannot enter the city of Hastinapura until our time of exile is over.'

'And then, we shall enter your city and perform a yagna where your king and all those who support him shall be slaughtered like sacrificial goats,' Bhima added, unable to contain his rage.

THE EXPLOITS OF JAYADRATHA

The twelfth year of exile dragged on and on and on. Yudhishthira was pensive as he contemplated the enormous suffering he had inflicted on his wife and brothers. After all the recent battles, Dwaitavana was no longer the peaceful retreat it had once been, and the Pandavas decided to return to the Kamyaka forest and stay there for a while.

In the meanwhile, Dushala, the youngest of the Kauravas and the only daughter, had been married to Jayadratha, the king of Sindhu. One day, when the Pandavas had gone out hunting, Jayadratha passed by their forest home on his way to the kingdom of Salva. There, in a clearing by the forest, he saw Draupadi standing by the doorway of their hut, one arm draped around the branch of a tree. Although he did not know who she was, he was struck by her beauty, which lit up the dark forest like a streak of lightning.

'Who are you?' he asked, completely infatuated by this apparition.

'I am Draupadi, the wife of the Pandavas,' she replied.

Jayadratha introduced himself. 'My husbands are in the forest, out hunting,' Draupadi said courteously. 'Pray be seated until they return.'

But foolish Jayadratha, smitten with love, proposed to the horrified Draupadi that she run away with him. 'I shall keep you in the comfort you deserve,' he said. 'You are a queen, not meant to live in the forest in this misery.' Ignoring her protests, he seized her and carried her away forcibly in his chariot. As they sped away, the deer scurried this way and that and the birds let out warning cries.

'Something is wrong,' said Yudhishthira. 'Let us hurry back to Draupadi.'

When the Pandavas realized what had happened, they set off in pursuit of Jayadratha,

who was naturally no match for them. Very soon, they had overtaken and overpowered him. The terrified Jayadratha leapt off his chariot and hid cowering in the forest. Nakula and Sahadeva rescued Draupadi, while Bhima taunted Jayadratha to come out and fight with him.

'Let him go,' said Yudhishthira, with his characteristic patience. 'He is our brother-in-law, the husband of our sister Dushala. It would be wrong to hurt him.'

But this time Bhima wouldn't listen. 'He has dared to abduct my Draupadi,' he roared and cut off Jayadratha's mane of curly hair with his sword. 'Return to your court and explain who did this to you and why,' he screamed, as his brothers tried to pull him back.

Sometimes pride makes a person detest those who have forgiven him. Jayadratha, like Duryodhana before him, was offended at the Pandavas' generosity rather than grateful for their forbearance. He was too ashamed to return either to Hastinapura or his own kingdom, and sat for a long time in the forest, praying to Lord Shiva. At last, Shiva appeared before him.

'I want to defeat the Pandavas in war,' Jayadratha pleaded of Shiva. 'Please grant me the strength and means to kill them all.'

Now Shiva never refuses his devotees what they ask of him, but this time he was forced to modify his boon. 'It is impossible to grant you this boon,' he said. 'The Pandavas are invincible in warfare. They are protected by Lord Krishna, who is an incarnation of Vishnu. If, however, you encounter the Pandavas without Krishna or Arjuna to protect them, you will, for that brief moment, be able to defy them.'

THE LAKE OF QUESTIONS

Once when the Pandavas were walking through the forest, a poor Brahmin came rushing to seek their help. A deer had stolen the arani, the fire-stick with which he lit the ritual fire. It is the duty of warriors to protect priests and holy men, and so the Pandavas went off in search of the deer. They roamed the forests for many hours until they were hot and tired and their throats were parched.

Nakula clambered up a nearby tree. 'I can see a lake not far away,' he said. 'I shall go and get us some water.'

A very long time passed, but Nakula did not return. Sahadeva went in search of his brother, but he did not come back either. Yudhishthira was worried and sent Bhima to look for them. When Bhima too failed to return, Yudhishthira sent Arjuna to find out what had happened. After waiting anxiously for a while, Yudhishthira set off after his brothers.

The forest was unnaturally still. Not a leaf stirred. There were no cries of flying birds, nor sounds of any beasts bounding. The crystal clear waters of the lake lapped at the shore. The bodies of the four Pandavas lay lifeless by the water. Arjuna was sprawled on the ground with the Gandiva bow beside him, arrows spilled over the sand. Nakula and Sahadeva lay as though asleep. There were no signs of injury on their bodies, but no signs of life either. Bhima's mighty form had fallen beside them, still as death.

Yudhishthira was shocked and terrified. He could not imagine what could possibly have gone wrong. Who or what could have killed his invincible brothers? 'All my hopes lie dead,' he lamented. 'How shall I ever face Draupadi?' His throat choked with unshed tears, Yudhishthira walked towards the lake to take a sip of water.

'Do not drink from this lake,' a deep voice boomed from the bottom of the waters. 'This is the lake of life: you can drink from it only if you can answer my questions. Otherwise, these waters shall poison you. Your brothers disregarded my questions and so they had to die.'

'Who are you?' Yudhishthira inquired humbly. 'No ordinary being could have killed my invincible brothers! Reveal yourself to me, O slayer of the Pandavas, and I shall answer your questions.'

'I am a yaksha, the guardian spirit of this lake.' A gruesome-looking creature appeared before the distraught Yudhishthira. 'I am pleased by your humility. Now I must ask you certain questions that you must answer before you drink of my waters.'

'Ask what you will, O yaksha,' said Yudhishthira.

The yaksha cleared his throat. 'What saves a man in danger?' he asked.

'It is courage that leads man through danger,' replied Yudhishthira.

'What is stronger than the earth?' asked the yaksha.

'A mother who brings up her children well is stronger and more sustaining than the earth,' said Yudhishthira unhesitatingly.

'What is higher than the heavens?'

'One's father is higher than the sky above.'

'What moves faster than the wind?' continued the yaksha.

'The mind runs swifter than the wind.'

'Who befriends a traveller?' asked the yaksha.

'Learning is the friend of he who travels,' replied Yudhishthira.

'What is the most valuable of all possessions?' the yaksha persisted.

'Knowledge is the most valuable of all possessions,' came the reply.

'What is the best form of happiness?'

'Contentment.'

'What makes one wealthy when it is discarded?'

'Greed,' said Yudhishthira.

'What enemy cannot be overcome?'

'Anger is that enemy,' Yudhishthira replied, after careful consideration.

'What is ignorance?' asked the yaksha.

'Not knowing or understanding one's duties is ignorance.'

'Who accompanies a man through life?' the yaksha asked next.

'His wife,' said Yudhishthira, his eyes filling with tears as he thought of Draupadi.

'And who accompanies a man in death?'

'Righteous conduct and dharma are one's companions in death,' said Yudhishthira.

'What is all the universe?'

'It is but air and empty space,' said Yudhishthira, a note of deep sadness in his voice.

'What is truth?'

'To see yourself in every living creature is truth,' said Yudhishthira.

'How may peace be false?'

'When it is enforced through fear.'

'What is more fatal than an incurable disease?'

'A false friend,' replied Yudhishthira.

'What is envy?' the yaksha asked.

'Envy is grief of the heart.'

'And what is grief?'

'Grief arises from not understanding the nature of the world.'

'What is true wealth?' said the yaksha, untiring in his questions.

'True wealth is found in the heart, for love and kindness are more valuable than gold, and honour more expensive than a treasury full of gems.'

'What is the most difficult thing to learn?'

'Restraint, and knowing when to stop, is the most difficult thing to learn,' said the wisest of the Pandavas, remembering how he had recklessly gambled away his kingdom, his beloved brothers and his precious wife.

'And now for my last question,' said the yaksha. 'What I ask is this. What is the most surprising thing on earth?'

Yudhishthira considered the question for a long time. 'All men know that they are mortals, and that death shall take us all,' he said at last, 'and yet, as we live, we delude ourselves that death will never come to us.'

'I am well pleased with your answers,' said the yaksha. 'You may drink of these waters, and as the water touches your lips, I shall grant you the life of one of your brothers. Choose which of them you want restored from the world of the dead.'

'May my brother Nakula be restored to life,' pleaded Yudhishthira.

The yaksha was surprised by his answer. 'Why did you not choose Bhima or Arjuna?' he asked. 'Bhima, the strongest of men, was dearest to your heart, and you depended on valiant Arjuna for victory in your battle against the Kauravas. Why then would you bring Nakula back to life?'

'My father had two wives, Queen Kunti and Queen Madri,' replied Yudhishthira. 'I love both my mothers equally, and so I ask only what is just, that a son of Madri should live as I do. I am the son of Dharma, and I seek always to follow the way of righteousness and good conduct.'

'Drink from these waters, and all your brothers shall live again' said the yaksha. Yudhishthira bent down to drink from the lake. As the cool water touched his lips, the four lifeless Pandavas stirred as though from a deep sleep and rose again.

Yudhishthira fell at the feet of the yaksha. 'You are not what you seem,' he whispered. 'No yaksha can possibly understand the question of right and wrong conduct as you do!'

The creature changed form. Dharma, the god of righteousness, stood in his place. 'I am your father, Yudhishthira,' he smiled. 'You are truly the son of Dharma, for you know and understand the laws of justice. I came here to test you, to see if you had learnt the difficult lessons life has tried to teach you.'

Yudhishthira was overjoyed. He had at last met the great god by whose values he tried to lead his life.

'I come to bless you, my son,' Dharma continued. 'Twelve years of your exile are almost over. In the thirteenth year, the year of disguise, your enemies shall be unable to recognize you. Go forth, Yudhishthira. Victory will always be yours.'

THE YEAR OF DISGUISE

In the twelve years of exile, difficulty and deprivation had taught the Pandavas much. They had learnt patience and fortitude. Arjuna had won divine weapons from his father and Lord Shiva. Bhima had been blessed by his brother Hanuman and by Kubera, the god of wealth. And now Yudhishthira too had met his father, Dharma, the lord of righteousness, and been blessed by him.

The brothers debated about where they might hide so as to be safe from Duryodhana and his spies. 'I know how our cousin thinks,' said Yudhishthira. 'He will seek us out in the kingdom of Drupad, or else in Dwarka, where he will imagine us to be hiding under the protection of our friend, Lord Krishna.'

Arjuna suggested the city of Virata, in the kingdom of Matsya. 'The king of Matsya is a noble and righteous man. Besides, he despises our cousin Duryodhana. We shall be safe under his protection,' he said. And so it was agreed.

They conferred about what new personas to assume so that no one would come to know their real identities during their year of agnaatvaasa or disguise.

'I shall become Kanka, a philosopher and companion to the king,' decided Yudhishthira. 'My knowledge of the holy books and scriptures should come in useful.'

Bhima resolved to go to Virata in the guise of a cook, and turn his love of good food to advantage. 'And I can train the wrestlers in his gymnasium in my spare time,' he added, his eyes lighting up at the prospect.

'But you shall have to contain your temper, Bhima,' Yudhishthira cautioned.

Arjuna's broad shoulders, scarred on both sides by the marks from his bow, the Gandiva, made him easy to recognize. Even strangers in far-flung lands had heard of the ambidextrous Arjuna, who could use both his right and left hand with equal ease to shoot his magical arrows. Arjuna's face crinkled up into a mischievous smile as they discussed his disguise. 'It's time to bring the apsara Urvashi's curse into action,' he laughed. 'Indra had suggested that I use it to disguise myself in the thirteenth year of our exile, and that's just what I intend to do.'

Nakula decided to work in the stables of the Matsya king, for he had a way with horses. It was almost as if he could talk to them and they would listen to all he said.

Sahadeva, the youngest, was as good with cows and cattle as Nakula was with horses. 'The wealth of the Matsya kingdom lies chiefly in its cattle,' he said. 'I'm sure the king will give me a job looking after his cows.'

Draupadi had decided to disguise herself as a sairandhari, a hairdresser and beautician. 'The queen of Matsya is fond of ornamenting herself. I will braid her hair for her and help her with her make-up,' she said.

The Pandavas looked doubtful. How would the beautiful princess of Drupad, the queen of Indraprastha, work as a handmaiden for an entire year? Yet there was nothing anybody could do about it.

But there was another problem to solve. 'What shall we do with our weapons?' the Pandavas wondered anxiously. 'Where can we keep them safe in the year of our disguise?' After much discussion, they finally hit upon a plan.

Arjuna unstrung his bow to hide it. His eyes filled with tears at the thought of parting with his most faithful companion during his years of wandering. 'No archery for a year,' he thought to himself. 'I don't know how I will survive it.'

They went to a nearby cremation ground, where the villagers burnt their dead. Wrapping up their weapons, including Arjuna's Gandiva and Bhima's heavy mace, in a shroud, they pretended it was the dead body of their mother.

'Oh, she was a wise old woman,' the Pandavas wept, 'and she lived to a ripe old age. Now that she is dead, we have to hang her shroud for a year from the highest branch of the tallest sami tree in the burning grounds, as is the custom in our land. Anybody who touches her corpse shall be cursed and die instantaneously.' The credulous villagers were terrified by this story and kept away from the weapons.

Yudhishthira invoked Indra, Varuna and Brahma, and all the other gods and immortals who had guided and protected them during their years of trouble. 'I beseech you to keep these weapons in safe custody until a year has passed,' he prayed. 'Let no one, not even our impatient brother Bhima, be able to reach them.' The gods assured him that they would honour his plea. Satisfied that their arms were safe from discovery, the Pandavas proceeded to Virata, the capital of Matsya.

The king of Virata held a public audience every morning at his palace. Yudhishthira introduced himself to the king at one of these. The son of Dharma could not tell a lie and yet he could not, under the circumstances, speak the truth. 'I am Kanka, a friend of Yudhishthira, the unfortunate king who is now in exile,' he proclaimed. 'I was closer to him than anyone in the world. And he to me.' The king was pleased by the stranger's noble bearing and dignified manner, and requested him to join his court as an honoured counsellor.

The others too all found the jobs they had decided upon. Bhima assumed the name of Valala and got employment in the royal kitchens, while Nakula, who called himself Damagranthi, secured work in the stables. Sahadeva, now known as Tantripala, was hired to supervise the feeding and care of the animals in the royal cattle-sheds.

Arjuna wore a long, red silk blouse to cover his broad scarred shoulders. Praying to Indra to help him in this difficult disguise, Arjuna assumed the identity of Brihannala, a eunuch. In those days, eunuchs, who are half man and half woman, would guard the women's quarters in the palace, where they would dance and sing to amuse the royal ladies.

The skills Arjuna had learnt from the gandharva king Chitrasena now stood him in good stead. Brihannala was employed to teach dance and music to Uttara, the princess of Matsya.

Sudeshna, the queen of Virata, was very taken by Draupadi's skill at hairdressing. 'There is only one problem, Sairandhari,' she said thoughtfully. 'You are too lovely and regal to be a mere maid. You look like a queen yourself. I am worried that my husband might fall in love with you.'

'I shall keep myself hidden from the king's eyes,' Sairandhari promised. 'I wouldn't like to cause any trouble. I have five gandharva husbands who have been separated from me due to a curse. They are very possessive and jealous, and would surely kill anyone who fell in love with me.' Queen Sudeshna agreed to hire the skilled handmaiden, and so the five Pandavas and Draupadi began the final year of their exile in disguise in the Matsya court. The months went by peacefully, and it seemed the thirteenth year would pass without anyone discovering them, when disaster suddenly struck.

KEECHAKA

Queen Sudeshna of Matsya had an older brother called Keechaka, who was commander-in-chief of Virata's armies. He was a huge, muscular man and a ready fighter, and the peace-loving king of Matsya depended entirely on him to protect the borders of his land.

One day, Keechaka came to visit his sister the queen in her royal chambers. Her new handmaiden's beauty drew him like a magnet. He admired her long, dark hair and large, flashing eyes.

Keechaka thought a handmaiden would be easy to woo with presents and big promises. He did not know that the handmaiden was actually herself a queen in disguise. 'I love you, Sairandhari,' he whispered. 'Live with me and I will keep you in comfort such as you have never known.'

He kept pursuing her in this way, pestering her day and night with his protestations of love. The proud Draupadi was offended by his advances, but she could not keep Keechaka away. Sudeshna, who adored her brother, was of no help at all. 'My brother is a handsome man,' she said. 'Why are you offended if he loves you? You are of humble birth, and he of royal blood—you must do as he says.'

Draupadi was disgusted by the uncouth Keechaka, who refused to pay heed to her firm refusals. In utter desperation, she went secretly to the kitchens and sought Bhima's help. Bhima's eyes became red as copper with rage. 'I shall kill him here and now,' he exclaimed, taking hold of a kitchen knife as he spoke. 'I shall kill him this minute!'

'Wait until nightfall,' Draupadi cautioned him. 'I shall lure Keechaka to come to the dance hall tonight,' she said. 'There will be nobody else there. You can teach him the lesson he so richly deserves.'

Keechaka was overjoyed when Sairandhari arrived at his quarters. 'I have changed my mind,' she said. 'I was afraid of my husbands, the jealous gandharvas. But you are too strong for them to trouble you! Meet me in the dance hall tonight, where we can be alone, and you will get all that you have been waiting for.'

Bhima dressed himself in women's robes and hid in the hall. Keechaka arrived, smelling of perfume, and wearing his shiniest jewels. In the dark shadows, he mistook Bhima for his beloved Sairandhari and leapt forward to kiss her. Bhima picked him up and twirled him around a hundred times before dashing him to the ground. Keechaka was dead and Bhima was satisfied that for once Draupadi's honour had been protected.

Keechaka's body was discovered the next morning. Nobody could understand who might have killed him or why. Queen Sudeshna was heartbroken. She suspected that Sairandhari might have had a hand in it. 'I should have known she was trouble the day I hired her,' she wept. 'Such extreme beauty always causes disaster and discord.'

Summoned by the weeping queen, Sairandhari confessed that her gandharva husband had slaughtered Keechaka. 'You must leave the palace before I destroy you,' the queen sobbed.

2

'Let me stay here a little longer, my queen,' Sairandhari pleaded. 'Only thirteen days remain before my time of exile is over. If you banish me, my gandharva husbands may get further enraged! They might even kill the king of Virata in revenge.'

The terrified queen had no option but to relent, for these fierce and mysterious gandharva husbands were clearly men of action.

The king was shattered by the news of his brother-in-law's death. 'Who will defend Matsya now?' he wondered. 'Who will keep my enemies at bay?'

Yudhishthira, disguised as Kanka, was by now firmly established in the king's favour. 'Do not worry. I know about warfare as well as statecraft,' he said. 'I shall protect your kingdom and your people.'

THE CATTLE WARS

All the kings and princes of Bharatvarsha were astounded by the shocking news of Keechaka's death. The commander-in-chief of the Virata army had been famous for his physical strength.

The Kauravas' spies had been searching for the Pandavas all of the year, but in vain. 'Only my cousin Bhima could have killed the mighty Keechaka,' Duryodhana concluded, when he heard the news. 'I am sure the Pandavas are hiding in Virata . . . and the beautiful woman that Keechaka is rumoured to have fallen in love with could only be that troublemaker Draupadi.'

Duryodhana sought the advice of Dusasana and Sakuni. They discussed tactics to provoke the Pandavas into the battlefield. 'Once they face us in battle, their disguises will be discovered,' gloated Duryodhana, 'and they will have to return to exile for another twelve years.'

When Dronacharya and Kripacharya heard of these plans, they were utterly outraged. 'Return his kingdom to Yudhishthira,' they counselled. 'He has righteousness and justice on his side.'

But Duryodhana could not be persuaded. Spurred by the jealousy and envy that fuelled his existence, he was set on the path of self-destruction.

'We shall attack the Matsya kingdom from the south,' he decided. 'We shall ally ourselves with Susarma, king of Trigarta, and get them to attack Virata. While their armies are fighting Susarma in the south, the armies of Hastinapura will surprise them in the north. They will face certain defeat and we can take the Pandavas captive.'

Susarma, king of Trigarta, had always been jealous of Matsya's prosperity and agreed readily to Duryodhana's plan. He coveted the herds of cattle that were the source of Matsya's wealth. With Duryodhana's support, his troops began looting and plundering Matsya territories.

The king of Matsya had always depended on his commander-in-chief, Keechaka, for the defence of his land. Now he turned in desperation to his trusted counsellor, Kanka.

'The wrestler Valala, who works in your kitchens, is a great warrior,' said Kanka. 'So are Damagranthi and Tantripala, who supervise your stables and cowsheds. I know them from the court of Yudhishthira; they are all able warriors. Together we shall lead your troops into battle.'

The Pandavas were once again in the thick of combat. The soldiers were inspired by their skill and valour, and soon began getting the better of Trigarta's army.

In the meanwhile, as planned, Duryodhana attacked the northern territories of Virata. All the troops of Matsya were busy fighting Trigarta's soldiers in the south.

When news of the fresh attack reached, only young Uttar Kumar, prince of Matsya, still remained in the capital city of Virata. 'I shall fight these invaders,' he declared grandly. 'I shall defeat them to the man.' But he could not go into battle alone, and there were no troops, no foot soldiers, not even a charioteer available to accompany him into battle.

He discussed his problem with his sister Uttara. 'I feel so helpless,' Uttar Kumar sighed. 'I want to fight the army of Hastinapura, but I cannot possibly do it alone! Even if I had a single charioteer with me, I would plunge into battle straightaway.'

Brihannala, who taught music and dance to Uttara, overheard this conversation. Arjuna had tired of his disguise and his broad archer's shoulders were itching for the feel of his beloved bow, the Gandiva. It had irked him immensely to see the other Pandavas rush into battle, while he was left behind in Virata to amuse the princess.

'I shall be your charioteer,' he said impulsively.

Uttar Kumar and Uttara examined Brihannala in surprise. They saw a tall, strong figure swathed in silk, wearing glass and gold bangles on sturdy wrists.

'I look quite different in battle gear,' Brihannala assured them.

'We have no arms or weapons,' stuttered the young prince. His bluster had quite left him and he was terrified at the thought of actually going into battle, accompanied only by Brihannala, who was clearly crazed. But he had no choice.

Ignoring Uttar Kumar's protests, Brihannala had a chariot prepared, and donned a gold breastplate over the silken women's robes. They made a strange spectacle as they rushed towards the battlefield, the man-woman with her flying robes and the child-prince with terror writ across his face. But Arjuna didn't care; he was exultant to be back in action.

►► ARJUNA IN THE BATTLEFIELD ◄◄

Uttar Kumar and his unexpected charioteer stopped at the burning grounds where the Pandavas had hidden their weapons. Arjuna revealed his true identity to the blabbering prince. A measure of confidence returned to Uttar Kumar, and he agreed willingly to Arjuna's suggestion that he take the reins of the chariot, leaving Arjuna free to fight.

They waited until dusk had fallen, and then Arjuna cautiously removed the shroud that hung from the tall sami tree. He unwrapped the cowhide in which the Pandavas' weapons were wrapped and kissed the Gandiva that rested among the glowing weapons. He took his quiver of never-ending arrows, and handed some weapons to the frightened prince.

Arjuna removed the lion-banner of the Matsya dynasty from the chariot and affixed the ape-banner of the Pandavas, which had been blessed by the monkey god Hanuman. The last day of the thirteenth year of exile was by now finally over, and he could declare his true identity in battle.

Uttar Kumar drove his chariot to face the assembled Kaurava army. Arjuna blew on his conch, the Devadutta, and let out a long, resounding battle wail which echoed through the land. Then he twanged the string of his bow.

The familiar sound drew mixed reactions from the opposing army. Dronacharya was secretly thrilled to find his favourite student safe and sound again. 'The brave Arjuna will destroy our entire army,' he told Duryodhana. 'It would be best for us to retreat immediately.'

'The thirteen years have not yet come to an end,' Duryodhana retorted. 'Arjuna and his brothers will have to go into exile again if they defeat us.'

Bhishma, the patriarch of the family, addressed Duryodhana sternly. 'My astrologers have been keeping track of the years of exile,' he said. 'You have done your sums wrong, Duryodhana. As the stars and planets move, the calculations of the years have to be adjusted. By our calendar, every five years there is an increase of two months in the calculation. During these thirteen years, there has been an increase of five months and twelve days in the leap years. The learned Yudhishthira surely knew this and has suffered an additional five months in exile to avoid any controversy. I declare that the Pandavas' time of exile is finally over.

'Return their kingdom to the Pandavas,' Bhishma counselled. 'Make your peace with them and your kingdom will be saved from certain slaughter.'

'The first rule of warfare is that an unnecessary battle must be avoided,' said Kripacharya. Dronacharya and Ashwathama too advised restraint.

Duryodhana would not be persuaded, and the hot-headed Karna sided with him.

'I will not return their kingdom to the Pandavas,' said Duryodhana. 'Let us talk of war and nothing else.' Bhishma and Dronacharya were silenced. In warfare, the word of the king is final and his commands must be obeyed.

'The king must be defended at any cost,' said Drona, looking at the anxious faces of Bhishma, Kripa and Ashwathama. 'Let us divide our troops into four. Duryodhana must

lead one contingent back to Hastinapura. The second will take the wealth and cattle we have won back to our kingdom. The other half of the army will remain to fight Arjuna.'

Arjuna saw his great-uncle's banner fluttering upon his chariot. It bore the emblem of a golden palm tree. The Kaurava army had arrayed itself into a diamond formation, the Vajravydha. Karna stood in the front. Behind him were Ashwathama to the left and Kripa to the right. Dronacharya stood in the middle of the phalanx and his grandfather Bhishma to the rear.

Arjuna's heart overflowed with affection at the sight of his teachers and his great-uncle. He shot two arrows which landed at Bhishma's feet; this was followed by another set of two unerring arrows which found their mark at Dronacharya's feet, and then again at Kripacharya's. This was Arjuna's way of paying respect and homage to his elders and humbly saluting them. Then a pair of arrows flew past Bhishma's ears, followed by similar sets of whispering arrows, which almost, but not quite, grazed the ears of Drona and Kripa. These arrows were Arjuna's way of seeking their permission to engage with them in battle.

All the three blessed Arjuna and were gladdened in their hearts by his humility. Ashwathama, too, was pleased by the respect shown to his father. Only Karna watched sulkily, glowering at his enemy, whom he had sworn to destroy.

As Arjuna advanced in his solitary chariot to take on the might of the Hastinapura army, he realized that Duryodhana was retreating and that the soldiers were herding the cattle away. 'First, let us release the cows,' he decided, and scattered the Kuru soldiers escorting the cattle with his unerring volley of arrows. As the calves began running this way and that in fear, the cows herded them back and turned southwards, to the city of Virata. The cowherds, who had been watching the battle from a safe distance, quickly led them back.

Arjuna asked Uttar Kumar to drive the chariot towards Duryodhana. The other Kaurava brothers, all ninety-nine of them, tried to stop him, but failed. Arjuna had eyes only for the chariot on which the banner with Duryodhana's emblem fluttered: a serpent embroidered on a cloth of gold. He was intent on daring his cowardly cousin to come forth and fight like a man. Still Duryodhana chose to flee when faced by the unrelenting wrath of Arjuna's arrows.

'Take my chariot to the centre of the battlefield,' Arjuna instructed Uttar Kumar once Duryodhana's chariot disappeared. 'I shall now confront Karna.'

The two men fought each other bitterly, but Arjuna held the advantage. Finally, as Karna's neck, shoulders and broad chest were covered with arrows from Arjuna's unending quiver, he conceded defeat.

Duryodhana returned to battle like a wounded serpent. Drona, Bhishma and Kripa came forward to protect him and surrounded Arjuna. The noble Pandava did not want to fight his elders. He summoned the magical astra called Sammohana, which had the power to hypnotize thousands at once, and all the Kuru warriors fell into a dead faint.

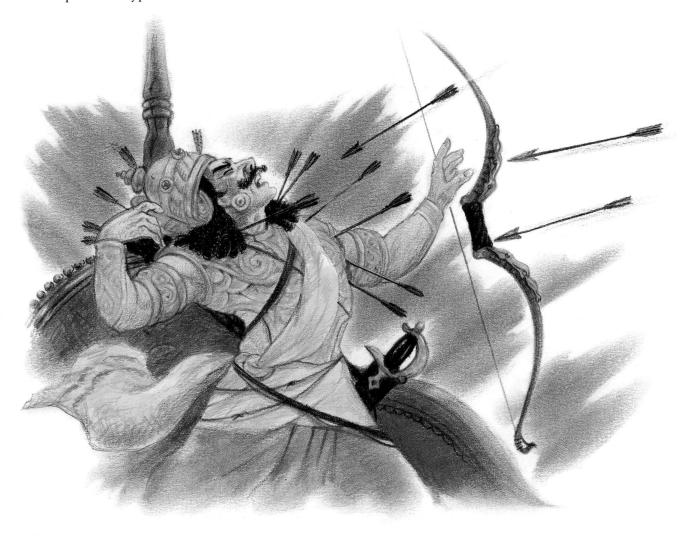

'They are all in a trance,' Arjuna said to Uttar Kumar. 'Get down from the chariot and collect their scarves and upper garments. Bring me Kripa's vastra of white silk, the yellow silk scarf on Karna's chest, and the blue shimmering silk on Duryodhana's chest. I will take them as trophies of war for my pupil, princess Uttara.' He paused, and a cautious look appeared on his face. 'I must warn you to keep away from my grandfather, Bhishma. He knows the antidote to the Sammohana spell; perhaps he is only pretending to be unconscious to humour me.'

For a warrior to be disrobed in battle was, in those days, the most absolute dishonour. After Uttar Kumar retrieved the scarves, he and Arjuna left the battlefield. Arjuna recited the mantra that reversed the hypnotic Sammohana spell. The Kauravas arose as though from a deep sleep and watched the departing chariot as in a dream.

Arjuna let loose arrows that fell at the elders' feet to express his respect for them. He said farewell to Duryodhana by aiming a magical arrow at his golden crown, which came tumbling down to earth. The Kaurava monarch's humiliation was complete.

They stopped next at the cremation ground, where the Gandiva and other weapons were returned to their hiding place in the so-called corpse hanging from the sami tree.

'You must tell no one of my true identity,' Arjuna told the young prince. 'You, and you alone, must claim credit for this victory. I cannot give up my disguise until Yudhishthira instructs me to do so.' The two exchanged places and the prince of Matsya was driven back to Virata by his charioteer, the eunuch Brihannala.

THE RETURN TO VIRATA

The king returned victoriously to Virata, having defeated Trigarta in battle. He was impressed by the prowess shown by his advisor Kanka, and by Valala the cook, Damagranthi the stablehand and Tantripala the cowhand. He had absolutely no idea that he had been assisted by the Pandavas, the greatest heroes in the three worlds.

When the king found that his son had gone off to fight the Kaurava armies on his own, he fell into a fit of utter panic. 'How can a young child fight Bhishma, Drona and Kripa, to say nothing of Karna and Duryodhana? My son will surely be sacrifed in the battlefield before such experienced warriors!' he lamented.

'But Brihannala is there to protect him,' Yudhishthira exclaimed, a little thoughtlessly.

'That dance master cannot protect my son,' the king said irritably. 'Let us sit down to a game of dice until he returns.'

'You should never gamble when you are perturbed,' Yudhishthira said soothingly, but the king was too agitated to heed this advice. They sat down before the dice-board.

In a while, some cowherds came to the city to give news of Uttar Kumar's victory. The king's heart swelled with pride. Yudhishthira, too, was thrilled by what he perceived rightly as Arjuna's victory.

'My son has achieved the impossible,' the king exclaimed.

'Your son is but a child,' Yudhishthira responded. 'Only Brihannala could have achieved this victory.'

The king was infuriated by this remark, which he considered an insult to his son. He threw the dice in his hands at Yudhishthira. The heavy ivory dice hit the eldest Pandava on the forehead and he began to bleed profusely. As the blood dripped from his forehead, he cupped his hands to stop even a single drop from falling to the ground.

Draupadi saw what had happened. She rushed towards Yudhishthira with a gold bowl filled with water. Yudhishthira washed his hands in it even while Draupadi wiped his brow with her scarf to stop the bleeding.

'Why are you coming to the aid of this foolish counsellor?' the king shouted at Sairandhari.

She looked up distractedly from her task. 'If a drop of this man's blood were to touch the ground, your kingdom would not have rain for a whole year,' she exclaimed. 'Each drop of blood will cause a year of famine. And if his blood falls on the ground, you will be avenged by the one who has sworn to kill whoever spills a single drop of this great man's precious blood. I am doing this to save you and your kingdom!'

Just then Uttar Kumar arrived at the palace. He knew that Kanka was actually the Pandava king Yudhishthira. He was utterly horrified to see him bleeding, and even more so when his father proudly informed him that he had hit his counsellor with the dice on account of his impertinence.

'You must seek his forgiveness, Father,' the alarmed prince pleaded. The king of Matsya was puzzled by his son's anxiety but did so, if only to humour him who had won such a splendid victory.

Brihannala entered the assembly hall. He had thought that his brother would smile at him, or perhaps give him a mischievous wink, to salute his victory. But Yudhishthira sat quietly, his face cupped in his hands.

That night the brothers and Draupadi conferred in secret. Draupadi told them how the king had hit Yudhishthira with the dice. They were all outraged, with Bhima naturally the most angered.

'Your patience has been your undoing all these years,' Arjuna said to his eldest brother. 'Let me kill this impudent king.'

'No, I shall kill him,' roared Bhima.

'He did not know who I am when he hit me,' Yudhishthira replied gently. 'Let him realize what he has done. Tomorrow, we will occupy his throne. If he resists, then we shall certainly destroy him and seize his kingdom.'

The next morning, when the king entered his audience hall, followed by his ministers and courtiers, he found Yudhishthira sitting on his throne, Draupadi by his side. The four other Pandavas sat around him, Bhima and Arjuna to his right, Nakula and Sahadeva to his left.

The king of Matsya was astounded by what he thought was the impudence of Kanka. 'Get off my throne before I kill you, you foolish man!' he screamed.

Yudhishthira smiled gently at him and said nothing.

It was left to Arjuna to reveal their true identities. 'This man who sits on your throne is Yudhishthira, the king of Indraprastha, monarch of the world. His fame will live on as long as the sun rises and sets. Do you still dare to unseat him from your throne?'

The king of Matsya was speechless with amazement. Just then Uttar Kumar entered the assembly hall. He had been longing to tell his father the truth, but Arjuna had forbidden him. Now he fell at Yudhishthira's feet and sought his blessings. 'It was Arjuna who fought the battle for us, Father!' he exclaimed. 'The Pandavas saved us and our kingdom!'

The king too fell at Yudhishthira's feet. 'Please forgive me, for I acted in ignorance,' he said, tears of remorse in his eyes. 'This throne and my kingdom are yours. I shall give my daughter Uttara to your brother Arjuna in marriage to seal our alliance.'

'We are grateful to you,' Yudhishthira smiled. 'We have spent the most difficult year of our exile under your protection. We do not want your kingdom, only your assurance that you will support us when we fight the Kauravas.' The king of Matsya agreed willingly.

Arjuna spoke next. 'Uttara has been my student. She is like a daughter to me. I cannot marry her myself, but I will accept her as my daughter-in-law. She shall marry my son Abhimanyu, born of Subhadra, and nephew of Krishna.'

Abhimanyu was summoned from Dwarka, where he had been living with his mother and uncle. The young couple looked at each other with love in their eyes. The priest Dhaumya performed the wedding rites. Kings and princes from neighbouring lands came to bless the couple, and to pledge their support to the Pandavas in the war that was sure to follow. Lord Krishna came accompanied by his brother Balarama, and his cousins, Kritavarma and Satyaki. Draupadi's father King Drupad came from Panchala, accompanied by his sons, Dhrishtadyumya and Sikhandin.

The shadow of the impending war loomed large, but the warriors celebrated and laughed and were glad for this short respite from the violent events of those difficult times.

KARNA'S GENEROSITY

Lord Indra knew that in the forthcoming war, Arjuna and Karna were sure to confront each other. He loved his son fiercely. Karna had both strength and invincible weapons, and had studied the art of war under the great sage Bhargava. Indra wondered how he could protect Arjuna. 'I will appeal to Karna's generosity,' he decided. 'Karna has a big heart; I shall use it to my advantage.'

Karna's father, the sun god Surya, came to know of the subterfuge Indra was planning. He was determined to warn his son and save him from certain disaster. At midnight, the sun god came to his son and spoke to him in a dream. 'The lord of the heavens, Indra, will visit you at midday, after you have said your daily prayers. He will come with his begging bowl, disguised as a poor Brahmin seeking to take advantage of your unfailing generosity and will ask you for your kavach—your golden breastplate, and your kundala—your golden earrings. You must not part with them at any cost. Promise me that you will do as I say.'

Karna was stubborn when it came to his convictions and oaths. 'I have made a vow to give alms at midday; how can I break it?' he asked.

'Offer Indra anything and everything you have, but do not give him your golden breastplate or earrings,' the sun god insisted. 'Your life depends on it.'

'I do not value my life more than my vow,' Karna responded scornfully. 'I have had a troubled and unhappy life. I do not mind losing it. If Indra, who gives life to the world, comes to me as a beggar, I will think it a privilege to grant him what he pleases.'

'Very well then, I will ask you for a promise. You must not refuse my request,' the sun god cautioned. 'If you are determined to be foolish and defy fate, you must ask Indra for something in return. Ask him for his Shakti, which is the greatest weapon a man can have. It may protect you and compensate to some extent for the loss of your kavach and kundala, which make you invincible.'

When the Pandavas had insulted Karna about his low birth during the archery contest many years earlier, Karna had taken a vow. He would pray to Surya at midday every day, when the sun was at its zenith, to seek strength to avenge the insult. After his prayers he would give alms; anybody might ask him anything, and he would grant it if it was his to give.

Karna was moved by Surya's concern for him. Nobody, except his foster mother Radha and his friend Duryodhana, had ever shown him any love. He had no idea who his real father was; neither did he know the identity of the mother who had so cruelly abandoned him in a reed basket in the river Yamuna after he was born. He did not know that Surya, whom he worshipped with such devotion, was his father. Neither could he dream of the strange circumstances under which Kunti had given birth to him, and to his arch-foe Arjuna. The entire story of the Mahabharata might have been quite different had these secrets been revealed to him earlier in life, but fate follows its own inexplicable course, and even if there is a reason for everything, sometimes we do not understand it.

A few days later, after Karna had finished his worship of the midday sun, a poor Brahmin stood before him with outstretched hands. It was, of course, Lord Indra in disguise. As expected, he entreated Karna to give him his kavach, his golden breastplate and his kundala, his earrings, as alms.

The rash but noble Karna paid no heed to the sun god's caution. 'I cannot be false to myself,' he declared. 'I must adhere to my vow and give you what you ask. But please listen to what I have to say before I grant it to you.'

Indra was moved by Karna's transparency and simplicity. 'Speak, my child,' he said.

'I know you are partial to the Pandavas,' Karna told Lord Indra. 'You wish to deprive me of my strength. I sense that perhaps I am not meant to win the war, for fate is not on my side. I do not seek victory or a long life. No, I seek only greatness. I will defend Duryodhana and fight his enemies, and do my duty on the battlefield. If you, Indra, the greatest of givers, ask me for my breastplate and earrings, you shall have them. They protect me, so in effect I grant you my life.'

Karna tore away the armour from his body and wrenched the earrings from his lobes. His face shone with an unearthly glow.

Indra's eyes were moist with unshed tears. 'You are the noblest mortal I have ever met,' he said to Karna. 'I bless you with eternal glory. Your name and fame will live on forever. Now I, too, shall give you a gift. Ask me for what you please.'

Karna remembered his promise to the sun god. 'Give me your astra the Shakti,' he said, 'and teach me how to use it well.'

Indra agreed. 'You shall have my Shakti,' he promised. 'But you can use it only once, against a single enemy. After that, it will return to me. May it serve you well.'

NEGOTIATIONS

War clouds were gathering. In Hastinapura, Duryodhana was intractable in his resolve to fight. Bhishma and the elders were vehemently opposed to war, but Karna, Duryodhana, Dusasana and Sakuni were all equally confident of victory against the Pandavas.

Yudhishthira sent an emissary to the court of Hastinapura. A learned Brahmin priest was deputed by King Drupad of Panchala to convey the Pandavas' point of view and to assert their right to get back their land now that their exile was over. In the meanwhile, the brothers were busy seeking the support of powerful kings and potential allies as they saw that war was inevitable.

In turn, the Kauravas sent an emissary called Sanjay to the Pandavas. The message he carried from Dhritarashtra amazed the brothers. Their uncle suggested that they forsake their right to the kingdom that was lawfully theirs and continue as hermits and exiles, for the sake of preserving peace. Yudhishthira's patience and forbearance had been interpreted by the blind king and his sons as sheer cowardice.

'Fire is not quenched when it is fed,' exclaimed the eldest of the Pandavas. 'My uncle, too, is like an insatiable fire; he is never satisfied, for his greed grows the more I feed it with my tolerance.'

The Pandavas took Sanjay around their camp at Upalavya, near Virata. He was shown their troops, chariots, horses and elephants. Then he was sent back to their cousins in Hastinapura with a clear ultimatum. Justice or war were the only options that Yudhishthira was prepared for.

Duryodhana's spies came to know that Arjuna was going to Dwarka to seek support from Krishna. 'Whoever has Lord Krishna on his side is sure to win the war,' Sakuni

urged Duryodhana. 'You must speak to Krishna before the Pandavas do. Rush to his kingdom without halting for a single hour on the way. You must forestall Arjuna.'

By the time Arjuna arrived at Dwarka, Duryodhana was already waiting in the palace. As Krishna was asleep, both of them decided to wait by his bedside until he awoke. Duryodhana strode arrogantly to an ornate golden chair by the headboard of the couch where Krishna lay sleeping, while Arjuna seated himself humbly by the feet of the man he revered and admired.

When Krishna awoke, his eyes fell first on Arjuna, and only after that did he realize that Duryodhana too was waiting in his bedchamber. 'What can I do for you?' he asked, a little confused at seeing the two of them before him at the same time.

'I have come to seek your help in the war that we intend to fight against the Pandavas,' Duryodhana said, in his proud, booming voice. 'As I came to you first, you must support me, rather than Arjuna.'

'We too seek your help in the war,' said Arjuna.

'Although you came here before him, my eyes fell first on Arjuna, as he sat by my feet,' said Krishna thoughtfully. 'One of you may have my armies and all the trained warriors, who form a formidable battalion. The other side can choose me, and me alone; but I shall not fight, nor shall I carry any weapons. Choose as you please. Arjuna shall have the first choice as he is the younger one and my eyes alighted first on him.'

'I choose you, my Lord, and you alone,' said Arjuna, his heart overflowing with faith and devotion.

'Then I shall have to be content with your armies,' said Duryodhana, who was secretly delighted by Arjuna's sentimental and impractical choice of an unarmed, neutral Krishna.

Krishna's brother Balarama had always been fond of Duryodhana, but he declined to fight for him. 'I cannot side with you if the Pandavas have Krishna with them,' he said apologetically.

Both armies were trying frantically to muster forces. In those days, a battalion was called an akshauhini. It consisted of 21,870 chariots, as many elephants, 65,610 horses and 109,350 footmen. It was important for both the Pandavas and the Kauravas to rally the support of their allies and get them to pledge their akshauhinis and other resources.

The Kauravas resorted to low tricks to secure allies. Salya, the king of Madra and uncle of the Pandavas, left his capital with an army of one akshauhini or battalion of invincible fighters. On the way, Duryodhana met him and pretended to be one of his nephews. The wily Kaurava duped the king of Madra into promising him support. A warrior must always honour his oath, and so Salya found himself pledged to battle against the very Pandavas he had set out to help.

Hearing of what had happened, Yudhishthira went in secret to meet Salya. 'You have given your word to Duryodhana to support him,' the Pandava said to his uncle. 'But there is one request you must grant me. My enemies will ask you to drive the chariot of their ace warrior, Karna. When the time comes for Arjuna and Karna to fight their final, decisive battle, you must destroy Karna's confidence. You must caution him and put fear into his heart and destroy his morale. I seek this promise from you.'

The king of Madra loved his nephews the Pandavas, and felt that they had been wronged by their greedy cousins, the Kauravas. 'I will do as you say,' he promised solemnly.

The Pandavas' allies began to converge at Upalavya. The first to arrive was Krishna's cousin Satyaki, with his contingent. Dhrishtkatu, the king of the Chedis, marched to Upalavya with his akshauhini of soldiers, all raring to go into battle. The king of Magadha, Sahadeva, son of Jarasandha, arrived with an akshauhini of trained men, chariots and elephants, as did the five Kekaya brother-kings, with one akshauhini. King Drupad brought his sons Dhrishtadyumya and Sikhandin and his five grandsons, Draupadi's sons, who were hot-blooded warriors, as well as one akshauhini. The king of Matsya had an akshauhini of Virata soldiers placed at the Pandavas' disposal. Other minor kings, like the rulers of Neela, Pandya and Mahishmati, came with their armies, which together comprised one more akshauhini.

The Kauravas too were drumming up support. All the kings who had paid tribute to Duryodhana during the Rajasuya yagna came to his aid, including the kings of Avanti and Khamboja. Salya, the king of Madra, who had been tricked by the Kauravas into supporting them, had one akshauhini of men, as did Bhoorisravas and Kritavarma. In the final reckoning, eleven akshauhinis of soldiers on the Hastinapura side, flying the pennant of the Kauravas, stood ranged against the seven akshauhinis the Pandavas had managed to assemble.

As the preparations gathered momentum, Lord Krishna visited Hastinapura in one last attempt to avert war. He wanted to broker peace without giving in to Dhritarashtra's greedy demands. Vidura, Bhishma and the elders agreed with his views but Duryodhana, Dusasana and the impetuous Karna seemed intent on self-destruction.

'Remember my words, O Krishna,' Duryodhana exclaimed. 'Not even as much land as is covered by the tip of a needle will be surrendered to the Pandavas.'

Krishna laughed. It was a strange laugh, which contained anger and sorrow, contempt and pity. 'You have always prided yourself on getting what you wanted, Duryodhana,' he said, in a low, steely voice. 'Well, you wanted war, and now you shall get it.' He turned to Bhishma. 'When my uncle Kamsa troubled and tortured everyone around him, I killed him, although he was my blood relative. Mighty Bhishma, you must sacrifice Duryodhana, Dusasana, Sakuni and Karna for the greater good of the Kuru clan. Give them up to the Pandavas and make peace within the family.'

Vidura, Bhishma, Drona, Kripa and old king Dhritarashtra listened helplessly as Krishna's voice rang out loud and clear through the royal assembly hall. 'The wise say that, for the sake of the family, an individual can be sacrificed; for the sake of the village, a family can be sacrificed; for the sake of the community, the village can be sacrificed. Furthermore, for the sake of saving one's soul, everything can be sacrificed.'

Vidura sent for Gandhari, the mother of the Kauravas, to try to persuade them to see reason. Gandhari was a wise woman. She rebuked her husband and sons, and implored them to refrain from war. But their hearts were filled with pride and greed, and their minds were set upon destruction. Duryodhana came up with a wild plan to take Krishna hostage.

Satyaki and Kritavarma, Krishna's cousins who had accompanied him on the mission to Hastinapura, came to know of the plot. They rushed to the assembly hall. 'The Kauravas are planning to hold you captive!' they told Krishna.

'Are they now?' said Krishna quietly.

Krishna was no ordinary mortal, but a god living the life of a man, a reincarnation of Lord Vishnu himself. When he heard of Duryodhana's absurd idea, he began to glow with a strange light. His physical form grew larger and larger, and more and more luminous, until it filled up the entire assembly hall. All the gods emerged from this glowing virtual form. On his forehead stood Brahma, the creator. The lords of the four quarters, Indra, Varuna, Kubera and Yama, stood on his shoulders facing the four directions. The eleven Rudras looked out through his chest. Agni, the god of fire, glowed from his mouth. The twelve Adityas, the Vasus, the Ashwin twins, the Maruts, all were clustered around him. Arjuna, too, stood with the Gandiva bow held in his hand; Bhima, Nakula, Sahadeva and

Yudhishthira stood facing the terrified court of Hastinapura. In his multiple arms Krishna held his war-conch—the Panchjanya, his discus—the Sudarshan, and his invincible mace—the Kaumodoki.

Although many in the audience were struck speechless with fear by Krishna's divine manifestation, Bhishma, Drona and Vidura were spellbound by the sight.

Breaking the spell, Krishna returned to his human form. Bowing to the elders, he hurried to the chariot that was awaiting him. There were two more people he intended to visit before he returned to Upalavya. He first went to meet Queen Kunti at the palace she shared with her brother-in-law Vidura in Hastinapura.

'Give this message to my sons,' Kunti said to Krishna. 'They were born of the gods and now they must behave as true warriors. My blessings are with them.'

KRISHNA AND KARNA

The second person Krishna visited was Karna. Taking him aside, Krishna held Karna's hand in his and spoke to him from the heart. 'You are the bravest and most generous of men,' he said. 'Why do you endorse this evil war?'

'All my life, people have scorned me and mocked my low birth,' Karna replied. 'Duryodhana has given me his friendship. He has been unfailing in his support. Only two people have ever given me their love: my foster mother Radha and Duryodhana. I will give my life for them.'

'I commend your loyalty, Karna,' said Krishna gently. 'It is time for me to tell you of your birth, and who your true mother is. Know then that you were born of the sun god Surya. Your mother was a high-born princess. She is the mother of five other sons: they too are as brave and valorous as you are.'

Karna's breath was coming in short, tight gasps. His heart was beating as if it would burst. His eyes had filled up with tears, and his face was drained of all colour. 'Are you saying, then, that the Pandavas are my brothers, and their mother, Queen Kunti, my mother?' he asked, his voice trembling with emotion.

Krishna nodded.

'Why are you destroying my life by telling me this now?' Karna cried brokenly. 'I have always been scorned by those very Pandavas for my low birth! Now you say that they are my brothers and that I too am a high-born warrior. And yet I have sworn to kill them.'

'I shall take you to your mother and your brothers if you wish,' Krishna said to the weeping Karna.

'Kunti gave birth to me,' Karna replied, 'but then she abandoned me. The wife of the charioteer Adiratha found me and brought me up with love. So Radha is my mother, not Kunti. I cannot be false to myself or to her. My loyalty lies with Radha and with Duryodhana.' He wiped the tears from his eyes. 'Why have you chosen to tell me the secret of my birth today?' he asked Krishna. 'I know we shall lose the war, but I must fight beside Duryodhana, even if we are doomed. I have sworn to kill Arjuna and I shall not go back on my word.'

A golden glow, like the radiance of the sun, shone over the unfortunate Karna. 'I will be as constant in my path as my father, the sun god, is in his,' Kunti's eldest son resolved. 'We part as friends, Krishna, although we shall meet again on the battlefield. You must promise that you shall not tell my brothers of the secret of my birth until after I am dead.'

Krishna was saddened by Karna's words, but gladdened immeasureably by his inner strength and unshakeable resolve.

Lord Krishna returned to Upalavya and told Yudhishthira of the happenings at Hastinapura. 'You must be firm, now that war has become inevitable,' he told the eldest of the Pandavas.

'We shall fight,' replied Yudhishthira. 'My days of forgiveness lie behind me.'

Draupadi's brother Dhrishtadyumya was chosen as the commander-in-chief of the Pandava forces. All the troops and the kings who commanded them converged at the great field at Kurukshetra, where the battle was to be fought. A moat was set up around the Pandava camp and tents erected for all the kings.

The Kaurava army also began its march towards Kurukshetra. Duryodhana requested his great-uncle Bhishma to command his army.

'I love the sons of Pandu as much as I do the sons of Dhritarashtra,' Bhishma replied. 'I will not aim at the Pandavas when I fight, but I shall undertake to destroy their army.

Only Arjuna is superior to me in warfare—only he can defeat me and perhaps even kill me.' He looked thoughtful. 'There is another condition which I must impose,' Bhishma continued. 'Karna and I do not get along with each other—I shall fight only if Karna is not allowed into the battlefield at Kurukshetra.'

Karna had been listening to the conversation. He realized that Duryodhana did not know how to react, for he did not want to displease either his great-uncle Bhishma or his friend. 'I promise you that I shall not enter the battlefield as long as Bhishma lives,' Karna declared. 'The pleasure of killing Arjuna shall still rest with me, as your great-uncle has vowed not to hurt his beloved Pandavas in any way.'

Back in Hastinapura, Kunti was overcome with anxiety about the fate of her six sons. The hatred that Duryodhana bore for the Pandavas was equalled only by Karna's hostility towards Arjuna. 'I shall go to Karna and tell him the secret of his birth,' Kunti resolved. 'Perhaps I can stop him from fighting.'

Kunti knew, as did everyone in Hastinapura, that Karna worshipped the sun at its zenith by the banks of the Ganga at midday. She approached him just as he completed his prayer. It was common knowledge that the generous Karna granted any boon that was asked of him immediately after his meditations.

'What can I do for you?' Karna asked the gracious lady who stood before him. He had never met Kunti in his years at Hastinapura, but he could see that she was of royal lineage. And yet there was something naggingly familiar about her, as though he knew her very well indeed.

Kunti feasted her eyes upon her firstborn child, whom she had not seen since that day so many years ago when he had confidently challenged her other sons at the archery competition. 'You may or may not know me, my son, but I have come to ask a boon of you,' she said softly.

'I feel as though I have known you forever,' Karna said wonderingly. 'I know your sad eyes, your soft voice, your face—you are the woman in my dreams.'

Kunti was startled.

'Every night for many many years I have had the same recurring dream,' her son continued. 'I see a woman who is dressed like a princess, but her face is always covered by a veil. She bends over me and the hot tears run down from her eyes to burn my face. "I cry for the injustice I have done you," she says. "I can talk to you only in your dreams." "Who are you?" I ask her, always, but she disappears without answering my question.'

Kunti's proud head was bowed low in shame. 'I am your mother,' she said sorrowfully. 'You are my firstborn son. The five Pandavas, your brothers, were born much after you were.'

Karna's head whirled with many emotions, but dominating all was joy. 'This is the moment I have waited for all my life,' he cried, as he clung to the mother he had always longed to know. 'What is the boon you want of me? Your son awaits your command.'

'You shall make peace with your brothers and rule their kingdom with them—that is the boon I ask of you,' Kunti exclaimed.

A voice spoke within Karna's heart. 'Listen to your mother and obey her.' It was Surya, the sun god, pleading with his impetuous son to do what was best for him.

But Karna disregarded the voice. After the first moment of joy, his heart was overflowing with conflicting emotions. 'All my life I nursed my anger against the mother who abandoned me,' Karna said. 'But now that you stand before me in the flesh, my heart is filled with love and compassion. And yet, my beloved mother, I cannot grant you the boon you ask of me. The enemy of your sons and my brothers, Duryodhana, has been more to me than a brother. I cannot let him down. What has been written by the fates and ordained by the gods cannot be changed.'

'Do not kill your brother Arjuna in battle,' Kunti pleaded, her frail body wracked by helpless sobs.

'I shall spare your other sons, Mother,' replied Karna 'I shall not engage in battle with Yudhishthira, nor Bhima, nor Nakula, nor Sahadeva. But I have sworn to fight Arjuna and I cannot go back on my word. I shall either kill him or meet my death at his hands. Whatever the outcome, you shall still be the mother of five valorous sons!'

The two clung to each other again, as though in a dream. Drained of all emotions, Karna returned to the battle-camp, and Kunti made her way back to her palace. In the distance, the sounds of battle conches wailed and resonated through the fields.

BEFORE THE BATTLE

The river Hiranwati was the point of demarcation between the two opposing camps. The Pandava troops were positioned to the west of the Kurukshetra battlefield, while the Kauravas were facing to the east. The rules of warfare were duly declared and accepted by both armies.

The code of conduct laid down by both sides tried to ensure that every confrontation was between two equal parties. A chariot could combat another chariot, an archer another archer, a macebearer take on another macebearer in the battlefield. Two archers or chariots could not engage against a single foe. Anybody who withdrew or retreated from the battlefield was not to be pursued or humiliated. Nobody could be attacked unawares or overtaken treacherously from behind. The rules of Sankula Yuddha or single combat applied also to foot soldiers and the ranks of the akshauhinis. These rules of battle were to be strictly adhered to at all times, for warfare was a strategic game of honour, not a barbaric show of strength.

Before the war began, Yudhishthira stood on the battlefield and addressed the hundred Kaurava brothers. 'If any of you wish to join the side of righteousness, come to us. We shall give you all honour and respect,' he pleaded.

Only one person stepped over. Yuyutsu, a brother of Duryodhana, approached the oldest of the Pandavas. 'I shall abandon my blood brothers for the sake of dharma,' he announced. 'I shall fight with your troops from this moment.'

The blind king Dhritarashtra was visited by his ancestor Vyasa, the great sage who watched over the Kuru race. 'I can restore your sight to you, O Dhritarashtra,' he said, 'so that you may observe the mighty battle at Kurukshetra.'

But Dhritarashtra declined the offer. He knew already in his heart that his sons were doomed, and that certain death attended all those he loved. Instead, Sanjay, a kinsman of the Kauravas, was granted the gift of inner sight by Vyasa so that he might relay the news of the battlefield to the blind king.

Before the battle formally began, the field of Kurukshetra echoed with fierce battle cries. The call of trumpets, horns, kettledrums and conch shells rang through the air. The thump of a mace, the whistle of an arrow flying through the air, the sharp clash of steel against steel; these were the sounds of preparation as soldiers tested their weapons one last time.

A sudden silence fell upon Kurukshetra as Yudhishthira removed his armour and laid his weapons carefully upon the ground. Unarmed, he walked towards his grand-uncle Bhishma, and the other elders, including his teachers Dronacharya and Kripacharya and his uncle Salya, and sought their permission to engage in battle.

Bhishma blessed Yudhishthira. 'The battlelines are drawn,' he said, 'and we must fight. But you have conducted yourself righteously. Dharma is on your side, for the moral victory is already yours. My good wishes are with you.' So saying, he wiped the tears from his eyes and prepared himself for the great confrontation ahead.

Bhishma blew his conch and let out a fierce battle cry. It was the formal call for the battle to begin. In response, Arjuna took the holy Panchjanya and coaxed a long angry wail from the sacred conch. His golden chariot, yoked with white horses, had Lord Krishna as the charioteer. As Arjuna looked up at the gathered ranks of their opponents and saw

the elders of his family, the people he loved and respected, arrayed against him, his head reeled. 'I cannot fight! How can I hurt those I love!' he exclaimed, swooning as he spoke.

Krishna revived him and comforted him with these words: 'O Arjuna, you should not grieve for those you fight. A wise man weeps neither for the dead, nor for the living. It is only the body of man that is destroyed by his death, for the eternal soul is imperishable.'

'But this is my family! How can I think of killing them?' said Arjuna.

Krishna smiled with infinite grace and compassion. 'You say that you will not kill. Yet you must do your duty, and fight against evil and injustice. Weapons cannot hurt the soul, fire cannot burn it, nor water extinguish its undying light. The soul is eternal and exists forever.'

Arjuna was listening intently to Krishna's words. 'You are a warrior; it is your duty to fight a just war,' his charioteer commanded. 'Do not be weak of heart. Wipe your tears and do your duty. Enter the battlefield of life as you must.'

These words of Lord Krishna later came to be known and remembered as the core of the Mahabharata—the Bhagvad Gita.

The Pandava army had a difficult time on the first day of battle, for Bhishma, their great-uncle, was the most accomplished of warriors. Brave Abhimanyu, Arjuna and Subhadra's son, Lord Krishna's nephew, resolved to retaliate against Bhishma's attack. As the oldest and youngest in the family met in battle, the gods themselves came down from the heavens to watch.

Bhishma's aged heart overflowed with pride at young Abhimanyu's prowess in battle. The king of Matsya, whose daughter Uttara was married to Abhimanyu, came to the defence of his son-in-law, aided by his son Uttar Kumar and Drupad, Dhrishtadyumya and Bhima.

Uttar Kumar led a fierce charge against the king of Salya, who hurled a javelin at the heart of the young prince. The gallant Uttar Kumar lay dead, and his brother Sveta rushed to avenge him.

Just then, Bhishma appeared unprotected before Arjuna. Krishna urged him to aim his magical bow, the Gandiva, but Arjuna refused. 'When I was young, a naughty, dark-skinned child with curly hair, I would climb all over the noble Bhishma and dirty his silken garments. When I called him father, he would correct me, saying that he was better than that, for he was my grandfather. I am still that dark child with curly hair whom he loved, and he is still my grand sire. I cannot, will not, fight him in the battlefield.'

Bhishma looked at them, smiling. 'I bow to you, Krishna. I will be honoured to meet

my death at your hands,' he said. But Krishna had sworn not to fight, and he bowed back to the grand old man of the Kuru dynasty, whose flowing mane of white hair fluttered like a proud banner on the field of Kurukshetra.

When the sun set, the warriors disengaged from battle and returned to their camps. But as the battle progressed over the next day, Bhishma's unbeatable tactics routed the Pandavas again and again. The banner of the monkey god which fluttered on Arjuna's chariot was in retreat. 'We must fight Bhishma,' the Pandavas resolved, 'even if he is our great-uncle and the head of our family.'

Krishna was halted by a chariot upon which fluttered a flag with a blue lotus on a silver base. Sikhandin, the man-woman warrior who had vowed to kill Bhishma, leapt on to Arjuna's chariot as it rushed in pursuit of Bhishma. The patriarch's bow sang a song of death. Rivers of blood flowed on the field of Kurukshetra.

Bhishma stood smiling in his chariot, even as he rained a volley of fatal arrows upon his opponents. Whenever Sikhandin advanced towards him, Bhishma would turn his face away and engage with another opponent. 'I must ignore Sikhandin,' he had decided, 'for a warrior cannot fight a defenceless woman, even if she considers herself a Kshatriya.'

Sikhandin's whole existence was for the purpose of killing Bhishma. She blamed Bhishma for all that had gone wrong in her life. She had sworn vengeance and become a man and a soldier in order to fight Bhishma. But the patriarch would not fight back, for his code of chivalry forbade it. Bhishma had been granted a boon that he would die only when he wished to, and the aged hero had resolved to face death only at Arjuna's hand.

THE BED OF ARROWS

Finally, on the tenth day of battle, the mighty grandsire Bhishma, born Devavrata—son of king Santanu and the river Ganga—fell from his chariot. Arrows had pierced him by the hundreds until there was no place on his body for another arrow to rest. Even as he fell, he could not touch the ground, for the arrows held him up above it.

Warriors from both sides assembled before Bhishma. They came with bare feet and bowed heads, their armour and weapons laid aside.

'I am still alive,' said Bhishma, 'and I want a pillow for my head.'

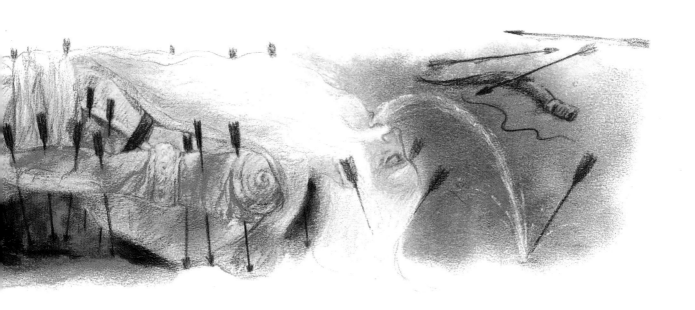

The kings and warriors hurried to do his bidding. They brought pillows of silk and cloth of gold from their royal tents, but Bhishma rejected them all.

Only Arjuna understood what he meant. He took his bow, the Gandiva, and shot three arrows from the magical quiver upon the ground near his grandfather Bhishma's head. Then he moved the wounded hero so that the feathered ends of his arrows supported Bhishma's mane of white hair.

'I want water,' Bhishma whispered next. The Kauravas rushed to do his bidding, but again he refused their offerings.

'Only Arjuna will understand,' he said, upon which Arjuna invoked the gods and sent an arrow into the ground near Bhishma's head. A clear pure fountain of water from the Ganga spurted to quench the thirst of her child.

'These are not Sikhandin's arrows that burn my body,' Bhishma said to himself as he lay on the bed of arrows. 'I shall die at Arjuna's hands as I was fated to.'

The royal physicians came for Bhishma, but he sent them away. 'I shall not die before the winter solstice,' he said, 'when the sun returns to its northern path. I shall rest here until then on these arrows.'

Soldiers from both armies built a trench around Bhishma, and sent guards to protect him; his flag with the emblem of the golden palm tree flew in the wind to mark the spot where he awaited his death.

Late at night, when the moon hid behind the clouds, Karna went to visit the wounded warrior. 'I am Karna, the man you so despise,' he said to Bhishma. 'I have come to seek your pardon for my anger and unkindness. Please forgive me, and grant me permission to fight the war.'

'I do not despise you, Karna,' Bhishma replied. 'You are a generous and noble man, and a great warrior. I know you are the brother of the Pandavas. I am honoured to have you as a grandson.'

'You must promise to tell no one of the secret of my birth,' Karna pleaded.

'I shall tell no one but Duryodhana,' said Bhishma. 'The proud Kaurava must realize the extent of your friendship and sacrifice.'

Karna went to Duryodhana's tent and conferred with him. 'The great Dronacharya, who has been your teacher, and is skilled in the art of war, should rightfully lead our army after Bhishma,' he suggested. Duryodhana agreed and requested Drona to succeed his injured great-uncle as commander-in-chief.

THE CHAKRAVYUH

Drona decided that it would be a good strategy to capture Yudhishthira. 'It can be done only if Arjuna were to be drawn away from his side,' he told Duryodhana. So a plan was drawn up. King Susarma agreed to lead the Trigartas against Arjuna. The Trigarta brothers—Susarma, Satyaratha, Satyavarma, Satyaasta and Satyadharma—challenged Arjuna and drew him and Krishna to the southern side of the battlefield.

The Kaurava army had been arranged by Drona into the formidable formation called the Chakravyuh. Duryodhana was placed at the heart of the circle. He was surrounded by the first layer of radiating petals: Karna, Dusasana, Kripa and other such fierce fighters. The next layer in the formation was composed of Dushala's husband Jayadratha, and his immense army. By his side were the heroic Ashwathama, son of Drona, and the brothers of Duryodhana.

The third circle was guarded by Sakuni, Kritavarma, Salya, Bhoorisravas and his brother Sala. The aged teacher of the Kauravas and the Pandavas, Drona himself, stood at the outskirts of this ring, ready to guard it with his life.

The Kaurava warriors were dressed in blood-red silken garments and wore fragrant garlands of scarlet flowers around their necks. Red is the sacred colour of victory. In the morning light the Chakravyuh looked like an enormous crimson lotus, blooming on the dusty earth of Kurukshetra.

Bhima led his army in an attack on the Chakravyuh. It was defended by Drona, who warded off the Pandavas with ease. Satyaki, Krishna's cousin, the king of Drupad and his son Dhrishtadyumya, Bhima, Nakula, Sahadeva, the sons of Draupadi, her brother Sikhandin, the Kekaya brothers; all these heroes could not make their way past Drona's chariot, with its prancing chestnut horses. Arjuna, the only man who was Drona's equal in battle, was fighting the Trigarta brothers to the south of the battlefield.

Yudhishthira turned in despair to sixteen-year-old Abhimanyu. Yudhishthira knew that Arjuna had been teaching his favourite son the complicated technique of breaking into the impenetrable Chakravyuh. Only four people knew how to do this: Krishna and his son Pradyumna, Arjuna and Abhimanyu. 'Help us to enter the Chakravyuh, my child,' Yudhishthira said to Abhimanyu. 'We must break down the defences of the Kauravas.'

Abhimanyu looked thoughtful. 'My father has taught me how to break into the Chakravyuh and enter it,' he said, 'but he has not yet taught me how to come out of it again.'

Now if the patient Yudhishthira had a fault, it was his rashness in the face of certain danger. It was this lack of caution that had led him to gamble away his kingdom, his brothers and Draupadi to Sakuni so many years ago. 'You need not worry about that,' he said confidently. 'Once you break into the formation, we shall follow you in and shatter their ranks.'

Abhimanyu's young eyes flashed with joy. 'My father will be proud of me,' he thought to himself. And yet he had a strange premonition of danger. Arjuna had repeatedly warned his son about how the formation closed as soon as someone entered it. To be trapped in the heart of the Chakravyuh, at the mercy of the Kauravas, was certain death.

Abhimanyu and his charioteer broke through the entrance of the Chakaravyuh and flashed like a streak of lightning to its centre. He was a great archer and skillful fighter, and he had all the weapons he needed at his command. Drona, Dusasana, Karna—the young boy circumvented all of them with ease.

Drona could not help but admire the valour of his favourite pupil's son.

'Drona is trying to protect Abhimanyu,' Duryodhana exclaimed angrily. 'We must destroy Arjuna's son.'

The rest of the Pandavas and their armies had failed to follow Abhimanyu into the Chakravyuh. They were held back by Jayadratha, the husband of Dushala, whom the Pandavas had routed when he tried to abduct Draupadi in the forest. Jayadratha had received a boon from Lord Shiva that he would be able to defy the Pandavas in single combat, provided that Arjuna and Krishna were not there to protect them. Now he invoked this boon. Neither Bhima, nor Yudhishthira, nor any of their forces, could get past Jayadratha to provide support to Abhimanyu.

Abhimanyu fought on bravely and steadily, battling kinsmen and friends he had known from childhood. He mowed through the ranks of the Kauravas like an angel of death. Rukmaratha, son of the king of Salya, died at his hands, as did Duryodhana's son Lakshan Kumar.

His uncles, the Pandavas, and their troops were nowhere in sight. Jayadratha and his elephants had blocked both their entry and Abhimanyu's exit.

Sakuni, the evil genius of the Kauravas, went to Duryodhana, as he grieved for Lakshan Kumar. 'It is impossible to defeat Abhimanyu in single combat,' he said. 'Let us all attack him together and destroy him.'

Forgetting every rule of chivalry and the just conduct of warfare, Dronacharya, Kripacharya, Ashwathama, Karna, Brihadbala and Kritavarma closed ranks against young Abhimanyu. Karna cut the string of his bow from behind him. Drona killed the horses that drew his chariot. Kripacharya killed his charioteer. It was six against one, and yet Abhimanyu fought on. Drona broke the hilt of Abhimanyu's sword and Karna shattered his shield. But Arjuna's son would not concede defeat. He grasped the wheel of his broken chariot and twirled it about his head like a discus. His young face glowed with anger.

'Fight me one by one if you can,' he exclaimed contemptuously. His opponents, all six of them, jumped on him and smashed the wheel to pieces.

Young Abhimanyu was trapped in a Chakravyuh he could not escape, and confronted with the brutality and treachery of his enemies. Tired and fatigued, he slumped to the ground. Dusasana's son rushed at him with a mace and killed the fallen hero. Abhimanyu's last thought was regret that Arjuna had not been there to see him fight his first and last battle.

AVENGING ABHIMANYU

When Arjuna returned to the Pandava camp after defeating the Trigartas, he knew immediately that something was terribly wrong. 'Why is Abhimanyu not here to receive me?' he said, looking around anxiously for his favourite son.

No one answered him. Only Yudhishthira's broken sobs cut through the deathly silence.

'I was told that Drona had arranged his forces in an impregnable Chakravyuh. Did you send my son into that deathtrap?'

No one had the courage to reply. 'I had taught Abhimanyu how to enter the Chakravyuh, but not how to escape it,' Arjuna said, looking accusingly at his brothers.

'We were certain we could defend him,' Yudhishthira replied with downcast eyes. 'But the Chakravyuh closed up behind him, and Jayadratha blocked our passage.'

Arjuna was trembling with rage and grief. 'I vow that I shall kill Jayadratha before sunset tomorrow,' he declared. 'No force in the world can stop me from avenging my son.'

There was rejoicing in the Kaurava camp. 'We have finally destroyed the might of the Pandavas,' Duryodhana yelled triumphantly. 'Arjuna will never recover from this shock.'

Just then, Arjuna twanged his Gandiva and Lord Krishna blew upon his conch, the Panchjanya. It was a renewed declaration of war, a message from the Pandavas that they would not concede defeat.

Duryodhana's spies returned from the enemy camp and told him of Arjuna's oath to kill Jayadratha before the next sunset. Jayadratha, not a brave man at the best of times, was terrified. 'I shall run away from the battlefield,' he stuttered. 'Let me concede defeat and retreat to my kingdom. I don't want to die at Arjuna's hands.'

Duryodhana and Drona promised to protect the shaken Jayadratha. Drona constructed an even more formidable military formation, with the Chakravyuh at its centre but reinforced further.

The following day, Arjuna, fuelled by an overpowering anger at Abhimanyu's death, penetrated the Kaurava defences with ease. Arjuna encountered his old teacher Dronacharya. The two were perfectly matched, and could anticipate each other's every move as they sparred and grappled on the fields of Kurukshetra. Finally Arjuna slipped past Dronacharya, for he had to keep his word and kill Jayadratha by sunset. It was approaching the winter solstice when the sun sets early in the evening.

Arjuna had resolved to use the Pasupata, the divine weapon he had received from Lord Shiva, to avenge his son's death. But the shadows were lengthening, and time was running out. 'The sun will set in a few moments,' Krishna murmured to Arjuna. 'When I instruct you, you must aim the Pasupata at Jayadratha without questioning me.'

Using the magical powers of illusion, Krishna caused darkness to descend upon the battlefield of Kurukshetra. Thinking the time of battle to be over, the jubilant Kauravas threw down their arms and began cheering.

'Jayadratha is looking at the dark sky,' Krishna said to Arjuna. 'Aim the Pasupata at him and avenge Abhimanyu's death.'

The Pasupata cut off Jayadratha's head and severed it from his body. The darkness lifted and the sun shone again. Krishna instructed Arjuna to recite a magical incantation that caused the decapitated head to float from Kurukshetra across the fields and forests into the lap of Jayadratha's father, Vriddhakshatra, who was saying his evening prayers. As he stood up after his prayers, his son's head rolled into his lap. In an explosion that could be heard all the way to distant Kurukshetra, Jayadratha's father burst into a ball of fire.

Arjuna recited the incantation to recall the mighty Pasupata. It came back, borne by a cool perfumed breeze.

As Krishna hurried their chariot back to the camp, he told Arjuna of the curse that Jayadratha's father had once invoked on whoever killed his son. 'Whoever caused Jayadratha's head to fall to the earth was ordained to die,' Krishna explained. 'I had to protect you, so I returned his head to his father.'

The battle in the field of Kurukshetra continued on its fated course. Duryodhana was dejected by his brother-in-law's death; Dushala, the only sister of the hundred Kaurava brothers, was now a widow. Jayadratha's death only strengthened Dronacharya's resolve to win the battle and hardened his heart against his Pandava pupils. His keen eyes watched and observed every corner of the battlefield, even as he planned swift strategies and counter-strategies to outwit the nimble Pandavas and their determined allies.

Now that Arjuna had honoured his vow to slay Abhimanyu's killer, Yudhishthira made a renewed effort to decimate Duryodhana's disheartened troops.

GHATOTKACHA

Ghatotkacha, Bhima's son born of the demoness Hidimbi, came from his forest home to assist his father and uncles in battle. He was a young man of heroic strength and power. His war cries sent shivers of fear through the Kaurava camp, and his savage team of rakshasas were almost invincible.

Ghatotkacha's first memorable encounter was with Ashwathama. Bhima's son used the power of magical delusion to confuse his enemy, but Ashwathama countered him with his vast armoury of divine astras.

The powers of rakshasas increase in the dark of night. Breaking all the rules of warfare, the battle between Ghatotkacha and Ashwathama continued late into the hours of magical darkness.

Karna came to the rescue of the Kaurava army. He fought bravely, but his unwavering aim was of no use in the face of Ghatotkacha's powers of illusion. Ghatotkacha would change his form at will and so Karna's arrows could never find their target. When he rained stones on the Kaurava army, Karna countered it with the Yayavyastra. When he sent out a huge raincloud that dripped lethal arrows, Karna let loose his Aindrastra. The Kaurava army was speechless with terror. Karna realized that unless he acted immediately, they might surrender to the Pandavas. He decided to use the Shakti, the weapon given to him by Lord Indra in return for his invincible golden breastplate and earrings. He had reserved the Shakti for his final and decisive encounter with Arjuna, but now he had no option but to employ it to counter Ghatotkacha. The Shakti streaked across the sky at the speed of lightning, piercing the cloak of illusion with which Ghatotkacha defended himself. Bhima's son fell to earth, but even as he died he summoned his magical powers one last time. His body swelled and grew until it was an enormous, heavy mass, and as it landed on the Kaurava army it destroyed one entire akshauhini with the impact of its fall.

Bhima felt his heart would break. The price of the war was higher than what even this bravest of warriors could bear. His beloved firstborn son, Ghatotkacha, was dead. Even

as Bhima grieved, Krishna smiled an inscrutable smile. He knew, now that Karna had used the Shakti, his favourite cousin Arjuna was safe.

Karna, too, was depressed and disheartened. His fate was sealed. The desperate measures that had dictated the premature use of his ultimate weapon had spelt out his own doom.

Draupadi's father, King Drupad of Panchala, charged forward towards Dronacharya, his heart bitter with anger and revenge. Many many years ago, at the hermitage of the sage Bharadwaja, Drona had been Drupad's friend and companion. But since then this old friendship had turned to enmity. Drupad had humbled Drona when he came seeking help. In turn, Drona had instructed his students to capture Drupad. Arjuna had won half of Drupad's kingdom for his teacher, and held his future father-in-law captive. Drupad had vowed revenge on Drona then; now his sons-in-law were arrayed in battle against their former teacher.

Lost in thought, his heart overcome with memories, Drupad barely registered the fatal golden arrow winged with blue feathers that whizzed at him from Drona's copper and gold chariot. Drupad fell, and for a moment Drona too felt the weight of his years, and shed a silent tear for the man who had once been his dearest friend, when the world was young and innocent. His will faltered, and as he wiped his eyes dry and readied himself once again for battle, Drupad's son Dhrishtadyumya rushed towards him like the personification of death himself.

All those years ago, when Drupad of Panchala first had sworn vengeance on his childhood friend Drona, he had secured two boons from Lord Shiva: that he beget a daughter who would marry the valiant Arjuna and a son who would destroy the proud Dronacharya. Now it was time for his second prayer to be granted.

Dhrishtadyumya invoked the gods and prepared to avenge his father's death. His red banner fluttered in the furious breeze, and his dark shield with its hundred silver moons glinted and glittered with the force of his resolve.

Dronacharya's eighty-five years in the world did not burden him in battle against his younger adversary. His bloodshot eyes were still as keen as a hawk's, and his silver brows and long silver beard only added to the fierceness of his appearance. As the young man and the old acharya battled furiously, it became clear to all the assembled armies that Dronacharya was getting the better of his adversary.

Of all the brothers, Bhima loved Draupadi the most tenderly. Her beloved father was dead. Now it seemed that her brother Dhrishtadyumya would face a similar fate on the same battlefield. Bhima decided that he would defend Draupadi's brother by whatever means he could. He conferred with Krishna and came up with a plan. It was decided that Bhima would kill an elephant that was named Ashwathama. Having done this, he returned to the battlefront to work through their deceptive ploy.

The code of conduct of warriors enjoins the truth at all times; but the truth is often the first casualty in times of war. Bhima's chariot raced where the battle was fiercest. 'Ashwathama is dead!' Bhima roared, to the consternation of the Kaurava troops. It was, of course, the elephant Ashwathama that had died, not Drona's son.

The mighty Dronacharya faltered in mid-battle as he heard Bhima announce Ashwathama's death. He could not believe that his son had died. He looked as though he had been struck by a thunderbolt. His eyes flashed with the most intense grief; so deep was his sorrow that there was no place in it for rage. The deadly short arrows which he had been about to shoot at Dhrishtadyumya fell from his hands. Slowly, very slowly, Drona took off his armour and breastplate, and put his weapons aside. His face was ashen; suddenly he looked every one of his eighty-five years.

'It cannot be,' he thought to himself. 'My son cannot be dead.' His conviction grew again and Drona returned to battle with renewed vigour.

Drona fought like one possessed. He used all the divine astras at his command, including the ultimate weapon of the Brahmastra, which he flung at Arjuna, once his favourite pupil. The sky grew dark and the earth herself quaked in fear; but Arjuna knew the secrets of the Brahmastra. He too invoked the mantras that set loose a second Brahmastra: the two divine weapons met in mid-air and destroyed each other.

'Ashwathama is dead,' Bhima proclaimed again.

Drona turned to Yudhishthira. 'Does my son live?' he asked him. He was certain that Yudhishthira would never tell a lie.

'Ashwathama is dead,' replied Yudhishthira, and then, softly, under his breath, he added in a whisper so low that no one could hear, 'The elephant Ashwathama is dead.'

It was the first and last untruth that Yudhishthira, that most righteous of men, told in his life on earth. Yudhishthira's chariot, which had always floated a few inches above the ground because of his moral strength and dharma, came abruptly down to earth. The eldest Pandava had stolen an unfair advantage over his adversary. He had compromised himself.

Drona could never think that Yudhishthira might tell a lie like any ordinary mortal. Ashwathama was dead. Everything seemed meaningless in the face of that fact. Drona had lost the will to fight, or indeed to live.

'Ashwathama is dead,' roared Bhima again. The Pandavas' troops let out a feeble cheer, for secretly most of them had always respected and admired Drona's valiant son.

Dhrishtadyumya charged on, like an enraged bull, quite oblivious to the fact that his foe was unarmed and had ceased to fight. There was the sharp swish of sword cutting through flesh; Dhrishtadyumya was covered in blood, and Dronacharya's severed head was held triumphantly in his left hand. Drupad's son, still mad with anger and vengeance, threw Drona's head into the ranks of the Kaurava army. 'A gift from the king of Panchala,' he screamed, as the troops scattered in fear to see their commander thus beheaded.

Arjuna grieved for Dronacharya with all his heart. His love for his beloved guru had not waned even though the tricks of fate had placed them on opposite sides of the battlefield. 'How did Ashwathama die?' he asked Bhima, his face drawn with sadness.

'There was an elephant of that name,' replied Bhima, 'whom I decided to kill. I do not know what Drona understood by my words or those of our brother Yudhishthira.'

'You struck him down with a lie,' reproached Arjuna. 'That is not the way a warrior should fight. Dhrishtadyumya killed Dronacharya when he was unarmed and heartbroken.'

In the meanwhile, Ashwathama had discovered his father's beheaded corpse. 'Who killed my father?' he asked Duryodhana. 'Who vanquished this invincible hero?'

When Duryodhana saw that Ashwathama was still alive, he understood the extent of their opponents' treachery. He went pale with grief and could not speak from anger.

Haltingly, Kripacharya and Duryodhana told Ashwathama of what had happened. 'They told him you were dead,' said Duryodhana. 'Dhrishtadyumya killed him after he had put down his weapons.'

'A valiant man lives on in the deeds of his son,' Ashwathama replied. 'I shall fight on,

undeterred.' He decided to invoke the secret Narayanastra with which his father had entrusted him. The skies darkened as he recited the terrible incantation: 'You are the silence of all secret things. Now break your silence and let loose the terror of your voice.' After washing his hands with holy water, Ashwathama let free the golden arrow that would bring about the destruction of the world.

In the Pandava camp, Lord Krishna observed the skies darken, and then the fiery rain of flaming golden arrows, all ten thousand of them. The heavens roared and rumbled, and the strength of a hundred thousand weapons combined in one will was let loose by Ashwathama to avenge the betrayal and death of his father.

Krishna realized that the weapon Ashwathama had unleashed was none other than the Narayanastra. Krishna and Arjuna were the very incarnations of Nar and Narayana; they alone could defuse its terrible lust for death. 'Fall to the earth and seek her protection,' Krishna instructed the terrified Pandava troops. 'You cannot fight this weapon even in your mind. Submit to the lord of death and he may spare you.'

Bhima, stubborn as always, refused to submit to Krishna's entreaties, for he considered it cowardice to bend before enemy fire. The combined force of the Narayanastra rained down on him and him alone. His golden breastplate reflected the flashing of a thousand suns. In desperation, Krishna's cousin, Satyaki, knocked Bhima down with a long wooden pole, and held him down until the might of the attack had subsided.

The gods and the immortals watched in horror as the enormous death-force of Ashwathama's final, desperate weapon held the earth hostage. Krishna smiled subtly and waited for the cloud of destruction to dissipate itself.

After a very, very long time, during which the armies of the Pandavas hugged the bloodied soil of Mother Earth and entreated her protection, the flaming arrows exhausted themselves. A strange calm descended over Kurukshetra and the stars became once again visible in the dark sky.

In the hour between day and night, the terror of the Narayanastra returned to Ashwathama.

Drona's son wept hot, burning tears for the father who had loved and tutored him, and whose death he had been unable to avenge. He remembered the time when he had wept because he did not know the taste of milk; he remembered how his parents, Kripi and Drona, had consoled him. 'Why do we fight this war?' he said to himself through clenched teeth. 'Why do the Kauravas and the Pandavas seek to destroy the rest of us in the whirlwind of their enmity?'

DUSASANA'S DEATH

Bhima and Dusasana engaged in a terrible battle. Dusasana's hatred for his cousin fuelled his bitter attack. 'I remember all the times we have defeated and routed you,' he jeered. 'You and your brothers lived in the forest like animals. If you do not die at my hands today, you will surely return there again.'

'If you remember all this, you must remember my vow!' said Bhima, his teeth clenched and his angry eyes red as burning coals. 'I have sworn to drink the blood spurting from your heart! No one can stop me from doing so!'

Duryodhana and his brothers stood as though paralysed while Bhima lifted Dusasana by the neck. He twirled him around a hundred times before dashing his body to the ground. Then he ripped his chest open and drank the warm blood that spewed out of his heart.

'Now my vow is fulfilled,' said Bhima, 'and the honour of Draupadi at last avenged.'

KARNA'S LAST BATTLE

The Kauravas were disheartened, their courage broken. Bhishma had been vanquished in battle, Dronacharya killed. Dusasana had died the most terrible death conceivable. The war was not going well and they could sense defeat and disgrace hanging like a shadow over them.

On the night of the new moon, Karna went under cover of darkness to the Pandava camp. There was no music or laughter in the camps, only fatigue and despondency. Physicians pulled out arrows and darts from the bodies of the wounded, and priests recited prayers and incantations to heal them.

Karna made his way stealthily towards Arjuna's tent. He wondered fleetingly how it would have been if things had been different, if he had received the love of his mother rather than being abandoned by her at birth. They might have laughed and joked and competed with each other in sport, rather than being engaged in a grim death-battle. All the hatred had been bled out of him, and the anger which had sustained him all his life had given way to a wistful regret, now that he knew who his mother and brothers were.

His appearance took Arjuna by surprise. 'Let us meet in the battlefield of Kurukshetra tomorrow,' Karna said to him without preamble. 'The time has come for us to fight to the finish. One of us shall live to see the dawn; the other shall greet his death.'

'Certainly, my honoured foe,' Arjuna replied courteously. 'Death shall meet you tomorrow at my behest.' Little did he realize that the radiant warrior he had sworn to kill was his blood brother, born from the same womb as him. Not even in his dreams could he have imagined that Karna was Kunti's abandoned son.

In the Kaurava camp, Duryodhana conferred with Ashwathama. 'Our troops need a commander to lead and inspire them,' he said. 'Ninety-eight sons born to Gandhari have all died at the hands of Bhima, while all the five born to Kunti and Madri continue to live. Only Karna, with his unparalleled valour, can save us now. Let Karna lead our troops.'

'Tomorrow, I shall fight Arjuna,' said Karna, trying to comfort Duryodhana. 'If I live, I shall vanquish the rest.'

'Then they are dead already,' exclaimed Duryodhana, for his faith in Karna was absolute and unflinching.

Karna was silent and said nothing, but in his heart of hearts he thought, 'I am doomed already to certain death; my brother is only to be the instrument of it.'

The next morning, the Kaurava priests greeted the dawn with sacred invocations and prayers for Karna's victory. Before he departed for the battlefield, where he was to meet Arjuna, Duryodhana came to greet him.

'I was the son of a humble charioteer when you anointed me the king of Anga,' Karna said to his friend. 'Today, I shall try to save your kingdom for you. I shall give up my breath and my body and all that I have for you. I cannot say if victory will come to me or to the valiant Arjuna; but of this I am sure, that I shall die your loyal friend and subject.'

'I think you have been beguiled by my treacherous cousins,' Duryodhana sighed. 'Dronacharya let Arjuna enter the Chakravyuh, and spared Yudhishthira from certain death. For his love, he was killed by a lie! Yet those whom the gods love ride on success whatever the evil acts they commit, while destiny defeats us at every step.'

The friends were both silent for a while. Then Kaalla, the malicious spirit that leads mankind to death, distrust and disaster, perched himself on Karna's broad shoulders. 'Your destiny awaits you,' Kaalla whispered to the sixth Pandava. 'Forget this talk of omens and what is preordained. You shall kill Arjuna today.'

Karna's sad heart took courage again, and he strode into battle determined to destroy his brother.

The gods had assembled in the heavens to watch Karna, born of the sun god Surya, enter into battle with Arjuna, son of Indra, lord of the heavens. The skies above Kurukshetra were crowded with their anxious faces as they observed Karna string his bow, the Vijaya, which no man but he could bend. Arjuna, too, was caressing his bow, the Gandiva. The sun god's heart was heavy as he watched the scene from the heavens, for he knew that Karna's trust and generosity were the very qualities that had led to his betrayal.

The two armies gathered to watch this decisive encounter from a respectful distance.

Kurukshetra was covered with dead bodies, scattered with severed arms and broken legs and decapitated heads and other such emblems and tokens of victory and defeat.

Salya, king of Madra, had been chosen as charioteer to Karna. Only Salya could possibly match Arjuna's charioteer, the divine Krishna, in strength and strategy. It was another matter altogether that, unknown to both Duryodhana and Karna, Salya had promised his nephew Yudhishthira that he would help his kinsman Arjuna rather than Karna in this crucial encounter.

Karna had anointed his rugged shoulders with sandal paste. He wore a fragrant garland of sweet-smelling flowers around his muscular neck. Behind him stood a second chariot stacked with long supple arrows winged with dark feathers, to hold out against his opponent's magical quiver of unending arrows.

Salya greeted Karna with a gracious smile. Having gotten to know the generous-hearted warrior better, Salya now regretted his promise to the Pandavas. 'I shall be fair to Karna,' he resolved.

Lord Krishna harnessed the silver-white horses of his chariot and led Arjuna into the battlefield. When he sighted Karna, his eyes lit up with a deep compassion; and yet his usual inscrutable smile continued to play upon his dark face.

Indra hid his son Arjuna in a magical mist, but the sun god breathed hard upon Kurukshetra and blew the mist away. As the two brothers fought, death danced in balance between them. Their skill and courage were so well matched that it seemed they could both fight forever, neither conceding the battle until eternity. There was silence on the battlefield, broken only by the furious twanging of arrows.

Karna's chariot heaved and tilted over. The wheel was locked fast, mired in the damp and bloodied mud of Kurukshetra. Karna descended from the chariot to push the wheel free, but Earth herself conspired against him and rose to frustrate his attempt.

Arjuna took aim, and Karna thought, 'I must not die undefended.' He took up his

strongest weapon, the Nagastra, and aimed it at Arjuna's heart. His ultimate weapon, Indra's Shakti, had already been spent.

For the first time in his life Karna's unerring aim did not hit true. As his chariot had lunged down and was stuck in the mud he failed to calculate the distance accurately.

In Arjuna's chariot, Krishna pressed the wheel down so that it sank deep into the damp soil. The deadly weapon hit the golden crown on Arjuna's head and exploded into a corona of fire.

His hair was damp with blood, but still Arjuna lived. He aimed his Gandiva and flew a volley of swift and lethal arrows at his noble brother, beheading him. Lord Indra had beguiled Karna of his invincible armour, and now Indra's son had robbed Karna of his life.

The last ray of the setting son touched Karna's brow in benediction. Surya the sun god blessed his beloved son and sank grieving over the horizon.

THE DEFEAT OF DURYODHANA

His promise to the Pandavas fulfilled, Salya decided to fight the rest of the war like a true warrior. His empty chariot retreated from the field where Karna lay dead, his head with its mop of curly dark hair lying beside his body.

'I cannot believe that Karna is vanquished,' sighed Yudhishthira. 'A noble enemy commands respect even in death. I wish we had known each other in happier times.'

As for Duryodhana, who can describe his emotions? He was all alone now, and his world was falling apart. All his brothers were dead, and now the man he had trusted above all others to steer his army to victory was gone too.

The aged Kripacharya sighed and counselled that the Kauravas accept defeat. 'Death flowers are blooming in this bloodied field; let us sow the seeds of peace,' he entreated.

But a strange hungry desperation possessed Duryodhana. He smiled recklessly. 'Life is a game of dice,' he muttered. 'And I shall emerge once again the victor.'

On the eighteenth day of battle, Salya advised what remained of the disheartened Kaurava army to engage in a swift and sudden sortie. 'Kill them and run back from the fight,' he instructed the soldiers. Sakuni too was in battle-gear, playing the game of real life without his loaded dice to protect him. Sanjay, whom Vyasa had gifted with superhuman sight so that he could report the progress of the war first-hand to blind Dhritarashtra, was also conscripted to make up for the falling numbers.

In the field of death, Yuyutsu stood facing the army his brothers had once led, his banner of plain gold fluttering besides Yudhishthira's flag, with its emblem of a golden moon. Sahadeva's banner displayed a silver swan, and Nakula's a Himalayan sarabh bird. The banners flew proudly but the hearts of the heroes were defeated and weary of so much fighting. Only Yudhishthira, normally so gentle and patient, was resolute in his will to fight.

Sakuni advanced on a mountain horse, bearing a long silver lance in his elegant hands. His blue-grey eyes glittered, as always, with a sort of amused contempt. Nakula and Sahadeva leapt off their chariots and mounted swift steeds, one light and one dark, in pursuit. The great gambler had played his last game, and could not cheat the death that

awaited him. The youngest of the Pandavas together split Sakuni into three dismembered pieces, and left his body to rot on the battlefield.

Salya was dead, and Dhrishtadyumya relentlessly pursued the straggling remainders of the Kauravas' eleven akshauhini battalions that had swaggered into war just eighteen days ago.

Duryodhana, though wounded, was still alive. He fought alone, fearlessly and calmly, his arrows never missing their mark. Then his elephant fell, and he leapt off the mighty beast, first thanking it in death for the service it had done him in life.

With only a single mace in his hand as weapon, Duryodhana left the battlefield and wandered into the woods nearby. His body was burning with fever, and when he saw a tranquil pond he walked towards it tiredly and rested himself there.

Some hunters saw him and reported the news to the Pandava camp. 'We must find Duryodhana and end this war,' Yudhishthira pronounced.

They hurried to the pond where their cousin and foe had hidden himself. He lay hidden deep in the calm waters, away from the clamour of the battlefield.

'After destroying your family and kingdom, how can you hide in this pond and seek refuge from the consequences of your actions?' Yudhishthira exclaimed.

'I neither fear death nor wish to live!' Duryodhana replied. 'I have lost my friends and all those who stood by me. What should I fight for? The kingdom is yours to enjoy. Rule it well.'

'You had said that you would not grant us a needle-point of land,' said Yudhishthira. 'We do not fight for land or kingdom but for honour. We cannot let you go.'

'Then take me on one by one and I shall combat you all,' said Duryodhana angrily, his pride reasserting itself. He took up his mace against Bhima, and the two battled by the shore of the tranquil pond, far from the slaughter-field of Kurukshetra.

As Bhima faced Duryodhana, his mind filled with memories of all the wrongs Duryodhana had inflicted on his brothers and their beloved Draupadi. He had sworn at the time of Draupadi's public humiliation that he would break Duryodhana's thigh with his mace.

The two circled each other, trying to find an opening in the other's defences. Bhima drew Duryodhana off-balance, and hurled his mace at him. The jewelled mace, heavy with Bhima's anger, fell at his cousin's thighs. The king of the Kurus lay on the soft mud, immobilized. His body was broken, but his spirit was intact.

Bhima did a terrible victory dance, raining blows on his fallen opponent and stamping his head with his massive feet. Yudhishthira tried to restrain him. 'He is your cousin, and a king,' he advised. 'Pay him the respect due to him.'

'You have won the war by base tricks and deceit,' pronounced the dying Duryodhana. 'You killed Bhishma with a stratagem and Drona with a lie. The noble Karna was defenceless when you attacked him. You have not behaved as true warriors. As for me, I have had a full life, a royal life. My friends have loved me and given me their loyalty. I die only to join them, and leave the sorrows of life to you.'

So died Duryodhana, son of Dhritarashtra, the firstborn of the Kauravas.

Yuyutsu, the only surviving Kaurava, could foresee the destruction of his city, Hastinapura. The women of his kingdom had been widowed, the children orphaned. Only old men remained to defend them, and there was panic and confusion everywhere.

Yuyutsu sought Yudhishthira's permission to return to Hastinapura and establish order there. It was late in the afternoon when he arrived at the city of his birth. He first went to meet his uncle, Vidura.

Vidura's palace was deserted, and the sounds of weeping and lamentation could be heard in all quarters. 'Where is Duryodhana?' asked Vidura, his voice choked with sorrow. He knew in his heart that the eldest of the Kauravas was dead.

King Dhritarashtra had already heard the news of his son's imminent death from Sanjay. 'I weep for my sons, who I shall not see again,' he said, tears rolling from his sightless eyes. 'All my life I have been blind, and if ever I wanted the gift of sight, it was to see my sons smile at me. I am utterly destroyed.'

☙ ASHWATHAMA'S REVENGE ❧

After the Pandavas had left Duryodhana for dead, life had lingered within him for a while. Ashwathama, Kripacharya and Kritavarma went to see him, to pay their last respects. Duryodhana was in his final death throes, his long hair covered in blood and dust, his body a battlefield of life and death.

'I shall avenge your death,' swore Ashwathama before the dying king.

That night the Pandavas slept not in their tents but by the riverside, where the gentle river breeze soothed their conscience and the sound of the rushes swaying in the breeze was a balm to their souls.

Ashwathama went in the dead of the night to the Pandava camp, on the western side of the battlefield, near the Samantapanchaka lake. Dhrishtadyumya, the slayer of Dronacharya, lay asleep in his tent, unaware that death was stalking him. His nephews, the sons of Draupadi, slept in the tents surrounding his, as did Sikhandin, his brother.

The massacre was swift, and sudden. Breaking every code of Kshatriya honour, Ashwathama, Kritavarma and Kripacharya slaughtered the sleeping soldiers in the Pandava camp, and set fire to their tents.

'I have avenged my father,' said Drona's son, and they went to the pond where Duryodhana lay. Although defeated, life would not leave him. In this half-life, he heard Ashwathama's words as though in a dream.

'I have taken my revenge,' said Ashwathama, 'and the sons of the Pandavas live no more.'

'I die happy,' murmured Duryodhana and gave up his life.

At dawn, as the morning mists were clearing, the Pandavas returned to their camp. Only Dhrishtadyumya's charioteer had escaped the executioners. He told the brothers what had happened.

Yudhishthira wept, for his gentle heart could take no more pain, but Arjuna's eyes were dry and his resolution steadfast. 'Blood for blood,' he declared and went in pursuit of Ashwathama, who sat in prayer by the banks of the Ganga.

When he saw the Pandavas approaching, with Lord Krishna beside them, Ashwathama took a blade of durva grass and charged it with the sacred mantra of destruction. 'My father, Drona, taught me the Brahmastra,' he said, 'and cautioned me never to use it against mankind. But you Pandavas are not men—you are traitors, and vultures who feed on the dead. I shall destroy you and all your offspring, born and unborn.'

Uttara, the widow of Arjuna's son Abhimanyu, carried his unborn child in her womb. The Brahmastra first took aim at her and sought to annihilate the last remnant of the Pandava clan.

But Lord Krishna opened his celestial third eye and caused Ashwathama's weapon to retract. 'We have had enough destruction,' said Krishna. 'It is time to sow the seeds of peace; for the world to renew itself.'

Ashwathama, whom Duryodhana had anointed commander of his army before he died, conceded defeat and retreated to the forest to spend his life in prayer and meditation. Before he departed, he took the shining jewel from his headgear and gave it to the Pandavas as a token of victory.

GANDHARI'S CURSE

King Dhritarashtra went to Kurukshetra, where his sons, the Kauravas, had been slain. He was accompanied by thousands of weeping women and children.

Yudhishthira approached his uncle and bowed before him. The blind king gave his blessings, but in his heart there was anger and reproach. The other Pandavas also sought his blessings. After this, they went to Queen Gandhari and bent low to touch her feet and ask for her blessing. Since the day of her wedding, Gandhari had bound her eyes and consigned herself to blindness. Yet she could comprehend what was happening around her, and in people's minds, with her sharp intuition. Her hurt and anguish were so deep that even through the bandages tied around her eyes, her searing gaze fell on Yudhishthira's toe and charred it black.

Gandhari tried her best to compose herself. She embraced the weeping Draupadi, whose sons had all been killed by Ashwathama. 'We share our fate; our sons have departed and yet we continue to live,' she said.

'Forgive me, mother Gandhari,' implored Yudhishthira. 'Curse me with whatever fate you consider a fit punishment.'

'The Pandavas are my sons too,' replied the queen. 'Pride led to the downfall of my sons; I do not blame you alone, Yudhishthira.' Her tears soaked the bandages that bound her eyes. 'But you, Bhima, struck my son Duryodhana below the waist, against every rule of warfare! I find it difficult to forgive this. You drank the life-blood of my son Dusasana. Is this how a warrior should conduct himself?'

'Forgive me, mother Gandhari,' murmured the mighty Bhima. Tears were running down his face and he was weeping like a baby.

Arjuna saw Gandhari's anger and was stricken by guilt and fear. In his discomfiture he hid behind Krishna, whom Gandhari chose to address next. When she spoke to Lord Krishna, Gandhari's voice was gentle and calm, and yet it held a cold fury which made all who heard her tremble with fear. 'You are the one man who could have prevented this war,' she said. 'You are to blame for the death of my sons and the destruction of my family. Today I, Gandhari, wife of King Dhritarashtra, mother of the slain Kauravas, place this curse upon you and your Vrishni clan. Hear me well: thirty-six years to this day, your family and your kinsmen shall stand destroyed at each other's hands. Their wives and children shall weep and wail, as ours do now. This is the curse of Gandhari.'

Krishna listened to her serenely, a mysterious smile playing upon his dusky face. 'I thank you, mother Gandhari,' he said finally. 'The destruction of the Vrishni clan was preordained, but with your curse I shall no longer be the agent of its destruction. Curse me as you will, but spare the Pandavas your wrath.'

KUNTI AND HER SONS

Queen Kunti had not met her sons since the time of their exile, although Vidura had kept her informed of their whereabouts. Now, when she saw her patient Yudhishthira, her brave Bhima, her valiant Arjuna, her beloved Nakula and Sahadeva, her heart overflowed with love. But her secret grief for her son Karna was consuming her from within.

For three days Karna's body lay on the battlefield of Kurukshetra, where Arjuna had slain him. His wife lay weeping over his body, which even in death was radiant with the sun god's blessings.

All Karna's sons were dead, destroyed in the carnage. Since the world knew him only as the son of the charioteer Adiratha, he had no relative to say the death-prayers and perform the Kshatriya death-rituals for him. The noble and unfortunate Karna was as alone in death as he had been in life, from the time his mother Kunti had cast him to the waters and left him to his fate.

As Yudhishthira assisted Vidura, Sanjay and Dhaumya in the offerings to the dead to propitiate the souls of Draupadi's murdered sons, and as Arjuna said the last prayers for his son Abhimanyu, Kunti gathered up her courage. Karna had made her promise not to reveal the secret of his birth to his brothers while he lived. Now he was dead, and it was time for her to tell her other sons the tragic truth.

'You still have to say the prayers for one more brave and valiant soul,' Kunti said to Yudhishthira.

Her son looked at her with puzzled, uncomprehending eyes. He could not understand whom she was referring to.

'Karna was born a Kshatriya, a warrior. His mother was a young princess who feared disgrace. She was not married and yet she had borne a child by the sun god, Surya. This heartless princess, in her selfish concern for her own reputation, put the child afloat in a reed basket on the Ganga.'

'Who was this evil person?' Yudhishthira asked. 'Surely no mother could be so cruel!'

Kunti let out a choked sob. 'I was that mother,' she said, not daring to look her sons in the eye. Having finally revealed the secret she had been hiding all her life, she fell to the ground in a dead faint.

It took some time for her words to register. 'Karna was our eldest brother and we killed him,' Yudhishthira whispered brokenly to Arjuna.

Vidura revived Kunti, as the brothers tried to cope with the import of this new and dreadful knowledge. Lord Krishna watched them with compassion in his eyes.

'Did my brother Karna ever know the truth about his birth?' Yudhishthira asked Kunti.

She had recovered from her fainting spell, but the grieving Kunti was still too weak to speak. She nodded faintly. 'He knew,' she sobbed. 'But Karna made me swear not to tell you; he feared you would lose the will to fight. Your brother made me a promise before he died, that he would not kill any of my sons, except Arjuna.'

The Pandavas wished the earth would swallow them up. Perhaps the entire battle for victory had been a terrible, sad mistake: they had all lost more than they had gained.

Yudhishthira sighed. 'I remember the day I lost my kingdom at the dice game,' he said. 'I shall remember how my head was bent down in shame. I could see Karna's feet and in that moment I realized that they were just like those of our mother. At that sight all the anger had left me; I could not hate him any more. Oh, if only I had known that he was my brother, how different things would be.'

'Karna had me at his mercy on the day that Jayadratha fell,' Bhima recalled, and a deep sense of sorrow and shame flashed through him. Sahadeva and Nakula remembered how Karna had met them in a duel and let them go without putting up a fight. Yudhishthira now realized that Karna had honoured his promise to Kunti and spared him on the day he fell to Arjuna's dastardly attack.

'You kept this terrible secret from us, Mother,' Yudhishthira said sombrely. 'You did an injustice to your firstborn. From this day I curse all womankind that they shall never be able to keep a secret to themselves.'

THE DEATH OF BHISHMA

Yudhishthira was so disturbed by the injustice he had done to Karna that he lost all interest in his kingdom. He blamed himself entirely for all the bloodshed, and spent all his time in prayers and atonement.

Finally, Narada, Vyasa and the other great sages visited him and tried to make him see reason. 'The duty of a king is to rule, not to weep,' they told him. 'A king has no right to personal grief, for he lives only for his subjects.'

Yudhishthira saw the wisdom in their words and agreed to forget the past.

His coronation at Hastinapura was a grand and solemn affair, where old king Dhritarashtra crowned his nephew as the royal priests chanted their prayers. Krishna watched the ceremony with tears in his eyes, for it was the victory of justice and righteousness over injustice and greed.

Krishna knew that only the greatest of the Kuru warriors, the patriarch Bhishma, who lay dying on his bed of arrows, could instruct Yudhishthira in the art of governance. 'Yudhishthira, you must seek the blessings of your grand-uncle Bhishma,' he said. 'He alone can teach you what it truly means to be a great king.'

Yudhishthira was initially reluctant to visit the revered patriarch, whom he had defeated in battle. At last he overcame his hesitation, and Krishna, Satyaki and Yudhishthira went to the battlefield of Kurukshetra, where Bhishma held death at bay as he waited for the sun to change direction and begin its auspicious northward journey.

'Most revered of the ancients, you have but sixty-five days to live,' Lord Krishna said gently to Bhishma. 'I beseech you to use these precious days to instruct your grandson Yudhishthira on how he must conduct himself to be a just and righteous king.'

'I lie on my bed of arrows, my mind distracted by pain, my memory clouded by the unbearable events that attended the last days of my life. How can I instruct the mighty and victorious Yudhishthira, who is the son of Dharmaraj himself?' replied Bhishma.

Lord Krishna granted Bhishma a boon by which his pain and discomfort miraculously vanished. He was youthful and radiant again, as he had been when, as the young prince Devavrata, he had wandered by the banks of the Ganga.

The grand patriarch Bhishma taught Yudhishthira all that he had learnt of statecraft over the years. 'Justice and truthfulness are the marks of a good king,' he declared. 'His subjects must live in freedom and happiness.' He explained how the subjects must choose and honour their kings, how taxes should be levied, how the kingdom must be defended from covetous neighbours or treacherous courtiers. When at last he had transmitted his

treasure trove of knowledge and experience, Bhishma closed his eyes and took a deep, long sigh. He knew his end was approaching.

It was the month of Magh. The sun had changed its course and the time had come for Bhishma to die. Dhritarashtra, Gandhari, Kunti, the five Pandavas, Draupadi, Vidura, Yuyutsu, Satyaki and Lord Krishna all assembled at Kurukshetra to seek his final blessings.

Bhishma's face was lit by an unearthly radiance. The wonderful glowing light arose like a bird from his body and flew to the heavens above.

After Bhishma's body, on its bed of arrows, had been cremated, Vidura, Yudhishthira and Dhritarashtra took the ashes to Ganga, the river goddess who had given birth to him. She wept bitter tears for the son she had borne and who now had been returned to her.

A NEW BEGINNING

It was time for Uttara, Abhimanyu's widow, to give birth. Her unborn child had been burnt within her womb by the strength of Ashwathama's wrath when he had released the Brahmastra. The baby Parikshit was born lifeless. But the strength of Krishna's prayers returned Parikshit to life. In time he would become the heir of the Pandavas.

There was rejoicing in the household. After the long cycle of war and destruction, a young child had arrived to bring cheer to the family. Bhima, the tallest, fattest and strongest of the Pandavas, made a wonderful grandfather, and abandoned his warlike pursuits to hold baby Parikshit in his arms and make funny faces at him.

For fifteen years after Yudhishthira was crowned king, Dhritarashtra and Gandhari continued to stay at their palace in Hastinapura. Yudhishthira was always respectful and loving. Still, the aged king and his wife continued in their hearts to mourn their dead sons. Only Yuyutsu was still alive; he tried, through constant love and tender care, to bring some joy into his aged parents' lives.

As was the custom in those days, Dhritarashtra resolved to go to the mountains and spend his remaining days in prayer and meditation. Gandhari insisted on going with him, as did Vidura and Kunti.

Yudhishthira reluctantly allowed them to leave. He understood that they had seen too much pain, suffering and death; they took no pleasure now in the pomp and grandeur of court life.

Dhritarashtra, his wife Gandhari, his half-brother Vidura and his sister-in-law Kunti spent two years in the forest together, in the northern mountains. They lived in a simple thatched hut and wore garments of rough bark. They had no servants or courtiers, and cooked and cleaned for themselves. It was all very different from the royal life they were accustomed to, but they were at last at peace with themselves.

One day a forest fire swept through the high mountain slopes and Dhritarashtra, Gandhari, Vidura and Kunti were all consumed in the flames. The Pandavas grieved their loss. The long story of King Santanu, and his sons Vichitravirya and Chitrangad,

Vichitravirya's wives Ambika and Ambalika, and sons, Pandu, Dhritarashtra and Vidura, was slowly winding to a close.

THE DESTRUCTION OF DWARKA

After Kurukshetra, Krishna had returned to his kingdom of Dwarka, which he ruled together with his brother Balarama. The clan of the Vrishnis, so valiant in battle, had become indisciplined and pleasure-loving in peace.

When the sages Vishwamitra, Kanva and Narada came to Dwarka, the young men of the royal family decided to play a practical joke on them. They took one of their friends, a boy called Samba, and dressed him up as a pregnant woman. 'Can you please turn your third eye to the future and predict if this young lady will give birth to a boy or a girl?' they asked.

Now sages are not famous for their sense of humour. The prank was intended to embarrass Vishwamitra, Kanva and Narada, but the enraged sages gave way to their anger by cursing the Vrishni clan for all times to come.

'This man, whom you have dressed as a women, will give birth to an iron rod, which will be the cause of the destruction of your race,' they declared.

In time, Samba gave birth to an iron rod. The terrified young man rushed to Krishna and Balarama and told them of what had happened and of the curse of the three sages. Balarama immediately ordered that the iron rod be crushed into fine powder, which was then thrown into the sea.

Life went on as before. Only Krishna knew that Gandhari's curse and the prediction of the sages was inevitably bound to be realized. When the season arrived for the annual worship of Sankara at Prabhas-teertha, the entire clan set out for the journey together. Krishna had grown weary of the incessant quarrels and intrigues within the family. He knew already that this would be their last journey together, for he was powerless to fight the decrees of destiny.

Grand tents had been pitched by the sea. There was feasting and drinking and public games. One evening, when Satyaki and Kritavarma were drinking together, they began talking about the past, remembering old grudges and grouses. Satyaki had not forgiven Kritavarma for siding with Duryodhana in the great war. Now he insulted him, and called him a murderer for attacking the Pandava camp while they slept. Kritavarma, too, was very drunk. Old wounds festered within him and soon the two were brawling in public. Satyaki sprang at Kritavarma and beheaded him. Others joined in the fight, and when they had exhausted their weapons, they took hold of the long, stiff reeds that grew along the seashore and lashed out at each other.

Now these weeds had grown from the ground iron filings of the cursed rod that Samba had given birth to. In spite of Balarama's stratagem, the curse of the sages had fulfilled itself. The Vrishnis, whom none but their own race could destroy, had thoughtlessly and foolishly killed themselves. Only Balarama, Krishna and Daruka were still alive. Even Krishna's favourite son Pradyumna had been brutally murdered.

Balarama was nowhere to be seen. Krishna searched high and low for his brother until he found him in a wooded grove, leaning against a tree from where he looked with sad eyes at the advancing waves of the sea. Sheshnaga, the serpent who holds within him the coils of time, came from deep within the ocean to reclaim Balarama.

Krishna dispatched Daruka to Hastinapura to summon Arjuna to Dwarka. The widowed women and orphaned children were to be protected, and who could do that better than Arjuna?

Though Lord Krishna was an incarnation of Vishnu, he had been born in mortal form; he had to die as the rest of us do. He knew his time on earth was over. He thought of his childhood at Gokul where Yashoda, his foster mother, had brought him up so tenderly; his first and greatest love, the milkmaid Radha; the scene at Mathura when he had killed his tyrannical uncle Kamsa. He sat in the forest and thought of these things.

Just then the hunter Jara made his way through the thick vegetation searching for deer. He saw Krishna's foot and the yellow silk of his robes. Mistaking him for a forest animal, he took careful aim. He had a newly-crafted arrow, which he had made from iron he had found by the shore. Though he did not know it, it was part of the same rod that Balarama had ordered to be powdered and cast into the sea.

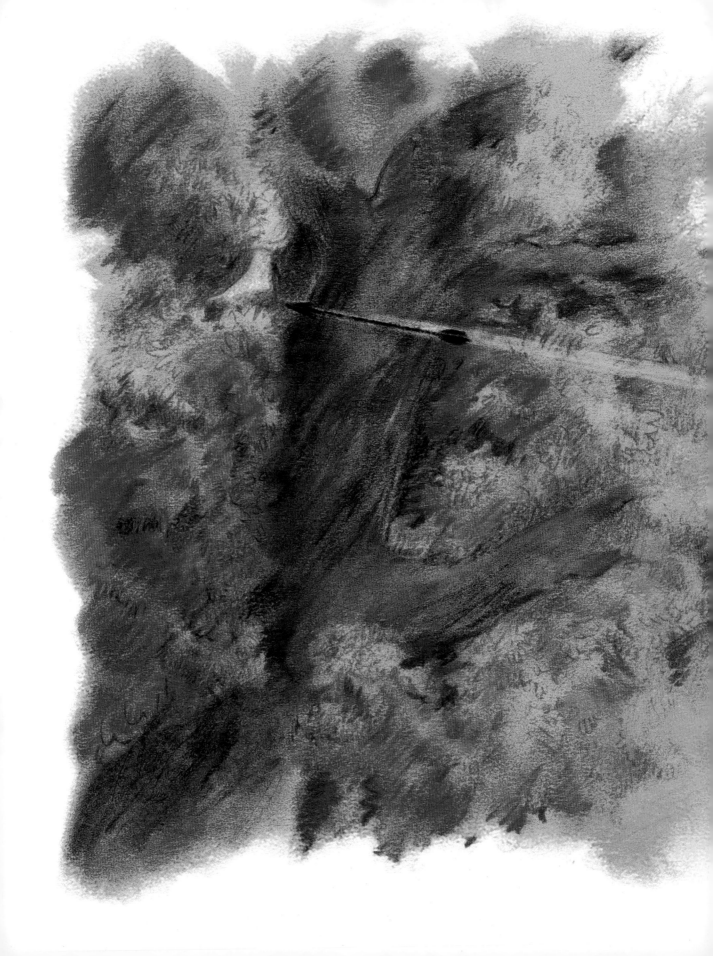

Long long ago, the sage Durvasa had granted Lord Krishna the gift of invulnerability all over his body, except in the soles of his feet. Jara's arrow pierced Krishna's feet, and went through his body, all the way to his head. He cried out in pain and Jara discovered to his horror that he had taken aim at the great Lord Krishna himself. Thus does destiny work its plans, overtaking our caution and good intentions. Krishna's divine soul ascended to the heavens, for his body had served the purpose for which it had been born.

Arjuna arrived at Prabhasa with Daruka in response to Lord Krishna's summons. He

found Pradyumna and Satyaki lying slaughtered among a field of mangled bodies. The two went in search of Krishna, but he too was dead.

Arjuna's sorrow was too great to be described in mere words. He set off with the surviving members of the clan—the women, children and a few old men—towards distant Hastinapura.

Dwaravati, the magnificent eight-sided city of gates, lay abandoned. The sea, which had taken Balarama into its arms, rose once again, a tower of water that lashed into the turrets and palaces of Dwaravati. Its deep roar was like a sigh through the heavens, and the salt water coursed through the streets of Krishna's capital. It submerged the beautiful buildings and palaces, and soon the city had sunk without a trace into the water. Time leaves nothing true, and not a trace remained of the grandeur of Dwarka.

🐦 THE WORLDS BEYOND 🐦

After Krishna's death, the Pandavas lost all interest in life. They decided to roam as hermits until they found their way to heaven. Parikshit, the son of Uttara and Abhimanyu, was crowned king of Hastinapura. The last of the surviving Kauravas, his uncle Yuyutsu, was appointed his guardian, and the aged Kripacharya, who had brought up the Kauravas and the Pandavas, was made his guru.

Yudhishthira was certain that he had left Hastinapura in safe and capable hands. He and his brothers renounced all they had, distributing their fine silks and jewels to the poor and needy. Dressed only in deerskin and rough cloth woven from bark, they set off on their last journey.

First, they visited Dwarka, or what remained of it. They stood by the seashore, contemplating the vast sheet of water under which the city lay submerged. There they paid homage in their hearts to Lord Krishna, who had guided them in the course of duty and righteousness through their years of war, exile and victory.

Agni, the god of fire, appeared before them. He addressed Arjuna. 'Long ago, I gave you the sacred bow, the Gandiva,' he said solemnly. 'I took it from Varuna, lord of the elements. The time has come for you to return it to him.'

Arjuna wept helpless tears at the thought of being parted from his beloved Gandiva. He took the magical bow and the quiver of unending arrows and returned it into the arms of the waiting sea. They sank without a trace. The serpent of time, the Sheshnaga, swallowed them up into his coils.

Next, they proceeded to the north, where the mighty snow-topped mountains of the Himavatha range awaited them. As they approached Mount Meru, Draupadi fell down in a dead faint. Neither Bhima nor Arjuna, nor any of the other Pandavas could revive her. Draupadi's years on earth were over.

Sahadeva died next, and then Nakula. Arjuna too fell before he could reach the gates of heaven, and then his brother Bhima collapsed beside him. They died before they could enter heaven, because they each carried some human frailty and fault within them. Draupadi was proud, and Nakula vain about his beauty. The wise Sahadeva had carried too high an opinion of his wisdom. Arjuna had fallen from excessive pride at his prowess in arms, as had Bhima for his incessant boasting about his physical strength.

Only the patient Yudhishthira was left to complete the long climb to the heavens. He walked alone, until a small, helpless puppy joined him on his trek.

The chariot of Lord Indra stopped beside the exhausted Yudhishthira. 'I have come myself to take you to heaven,' said Indra.

'I cannot come without my brothers or our wife Draupadi,' replied Yudhishthira.

'They have cast off their human forms,' smiled Indra. 'You shall meet them again in time.'

'And this little dog, who follows me so faithfully,' said Yudhishthira. 'How can I possibly leave him behind?'

'You stand at the threshold of heaven and worry about a stupid dog?' asked Indra scornfully. The puppy looked up at Yudhishthira and wagged its tail trustingly.

'I am the son of Dharma, the god of righteousness,' Yudhishthira replied. 'I cannot fail in my duty towards this dog because of my greed for the joys of heaven.'

At these words, the tiny puppy transmuted its form and stood before them in his true guise of Dharma himself. Yudhishthira bowed low to his father and received his blessings.

'I was only testing you, my son,' Dharma said. 'Let us proceed to heaven together.'

They reached the fabled city of Amaravati, which Arjuna had once described to his brothers from his travels there. Indra's palace was decorated with flowers to welcome Yudhishthira. All the kings and great men of the past had assembled to greet him.

But a rude shock awaited Yudhishthira. None of his brothers were there, nor any of his allies and companions in the war. Instead, Duryodhana was seated among the assembly of kings.

'Where are my brothers and all those that I love?' asked Yudhishthira. 'And why is the evil Duryodhana seated so comfortably in Indra's heaven?'

Narada, the celestial sage who knows all things past, present and future, came to his aid. 'Duryodhana was true to his birth and his duties,' he explained. 'He was never afraid. He ruled his kingdom justly. He died nobly in battle. The rules of heaven are different from those of earth and you must learn to accept them.'

'But where are my brothers?' Yudhishthira asked again. 'I must see them.'

The custodians of heaven took him across the bubbling, boiling waters of the Vaitarni, the river of hell. There was a stench of sulphur and rot and decay. Forms that might once have been human called out to each other in pain and agony. Yudhishthira could see and hear his brothers and his wife Draupadi, but they were oblivious to his presence.

The mists and vapours of hell vanished in a trice and Yudhishthira found himself back in Indra's heaven. He was not alone; his brothers and Draupadi sat around him, radiant with heavenly beauty.

'Every king must once behold hell,' said the custodian of the heavens. 'The best of men visit hell and then are transported to heaven, while those who have put their pleasures before their duties travel first to heaven and thence to the realms of hell. You, being entirely blameless and of irreproachable conduct, could have entered heaven without delay, but the lie you told about Ashwathama's death, even though it was a half-truth, cost you dear. This was the reason why you could not enter in all your glorious human form: for this lie, you lost your little finger.'

Yudhishthira looked down and saw that his right hand had only four fingers, for one had fallen off on account of the only lie he had ever told. And yet he was in heaven, reunited with his brothers and Draupadi and Karna. He thought of Lord Krishna, and in his mind he thanked him for guiding them through the difficult dilemmas of life to the reality of the worlds beyond.

And so, all the great heroes of Bharatvarsha who lived through those times arrived, after the dream of life, in heaven or hell or the dimension that awaits next. All this happened a very long time ago, when the world was young. The story has been told again and again, to generation after generation, as a caution against the evils of war, and a call to fight with courage and conviction when justice demands it.

GLOSSARY

DEVAS—THE LORDS

Agni: The lord of fire

Ashwins: The twin gods of dawn

Dharma: The god of righteousness

Indra: The lord of the heavens, also known as the lord of the east

Kama: The god of love

Kubera: The lord of wealth, also known as the lord of the north

Rudra: One of the forms of Shiva

Skanda: The god of war

Varuna: Lord of the elements, also known as the lord of the west

Vayu: The god of the wind

Yama: The god of death, also known as the lord of the south

DEMONS AND CELESTIAL BEINGS

Apsaras: Celestial women of incredible and everlasting beauty

Asuras: The enemies of the gods

Gandharvas: Celestial musicians, a class of demi-gods

Kaalla: The demon of wrong advice and misdirection or the Supreme Spirit regarded as the destroyer

Maya: An architect of the asuras who is said to have built a splendid hall for the Pandavas; in Vedantic philosophy it is unreality or illusion

Narada: The celestial sage who knows all things past, present and future

Rakshasa and Rakshasi: A class of demons

Sheshnaga: The great snake which is said to be the bed of Vishnu; it is also said to

bear the world on its thousand hoods

Vishwakarma: The celestial architect

Yakshas: Demi-gods or guardian spirits

EVERYDAY BEINGS FROM THOSE TIMES

Acharya: A preceptor, guru

Brahmin: According to the Vedantas, the Brahmin is both the efficient and material cause of the visible Universe

Kanka: Philosopher and companion to the king

Muni: A sage, a holy man, a saint

Rishi: A sanctified sage, an ascetic

Snataks: Brahmin students who have just finished their education under a religious teacher

Suta: A charioteer, usually an attendant of the king and at times even his confidant; a suta is the son of a kshatriya and a Brahmin woman

ASTRAS—WEAPONS (An astra is said to be presided over by a particular god who, when invoked, enters the astra)

Aindrastra: The astra presided over by Indra

Agneyastra: The astra presided over by Agni

Brahmastra: The weapon created by Brahma which is considered as the deadliest weapon that never loses its mark

Gada: The mace, favourite weapon of Balarama, Bhima and Duryodhana

Gandiva: The magical bow of Arjuna presented by Soma to Varuna, by Varuna to Agni and by Agni to Arjuna when the latter helped Agni to burn the Khandava forest

Kaumodoki: Krishna's invincible mace

Kavach: Breastplate, armour

Kundala: Ear ornaments

Nagastra: An astra presided over by a serpent

Narayanastra: Weapon unleashed by Ashwathama, it is the personal missile weapon of Vishnu in his Narayana form; this astra lets loose a powerful tirade of millions of deadly missiles simultaneously

Panchjanya: The famed conch belonging to Lord Krishna

Pasupata: Weapon given by Shiva to Arjuna; it is the irresistible and most destructive personal weapon of Shiva discharged by the mind, eyes, words or a bow, never to be used against lesser enemies and by lesser warriors

Pinaka: The bow of Mahadeva

Shakti: The weapon given by Indra to Karna

Sudarshan Chakra: The weapon given by Agni to Krishna, a razor-sharp discus with a thousand spokes and an iron rod through the centre

Vijaya: Karna's bow which no man but he could bend

SOME OF THE DHWAJAS AND CHINNHAS—FLAGS AND ENSIGNS

Arjuna's banner bore the emblem of the monkey god

Abhimanyu's banner bore the emblem of the beautiful mauve and white flower, the Kovidara

Bhishma's banner bore the emblem of a golden palm tree

Dhristadyumya had a red banner and his dark shield had a hundred silver moons

Duryodhana's banner bore the emblem of a serpent embroidered on a cloth of gold

Karna's emblem was a stout cord for binding elephants

Nakula's banner bore the emblem of a Himalayan sarabh bird

Sahadeva's banner bore the emblem of a silver swan

Yudhishthira's flag bore the emblem of a golden moon

Yuyutsu had a banner of plain gold

MILITARY TERMS AND FORMATIONS

Akshauhini: An army division consisting of 2,870 chariots, 21,870 elephants, 65,610 horses and 109,350 footmen

Chakravyuh: The circular formation of the army which Drona arranged during his commandership

Krauncha: The formation in the shape of the bird, Krauncha

Makaravyuh: The arrangement of the army in the shape of a crocodile

Padavyuh: The army arranged in the form of a full-blown lotus

Suchimukhavyuh: A difficult and rare arrangement of the army where the vyuha tapers into a needle point where there is maximum protection

MOUNTAINS, RIVERS AND GRASSES

Arani: A piece of wood from the sami tree; two pieces of wood are rubbed together to produce fire, specially the sacrificial fire

Durva grass: When it is dry, kusa straw is called durva or dharbai; however, some say these are two different species: kusa is *Poa cynosuroides* and durva, *Agrostis linearis*

Ganga: The celestial river which was later brought to the earth

Hiranvati: The river along whose banks was placed the Pandava army during the great war

Dwaitavana: The forest where the Pandavas spent a large part of their exile of twelve years

Kailasa: The peak in the Himalayas which is said to be the abode of Lord Shiva

Khandava: The great forest which was burnt by Agni with the help of Arjuna and Krishna

Kusa grass: Grass used in sacrificial ceremonies, the grass has been sanctified because tradition has it that the bowl of Amrita from the heavens rested on it for a few moments

Meru: Name of the fabulous mountain round which all the planets are said to revolve; it is also said to contain gold and gems

Sami trees: Tall trees with dense branches; the wood of this tree is used to make sacrificial fire

Vaitarni: The river of hell

Yamuna: The river which has been immortalized because of Krishna spending his boyhood on her banks; it is a tributary of the Ganga

YUGAS—Time is said to be divided into four quarters called yugas namely,

Satya: The first, where Dharma is believed to walk firmly on both legs

Treta: The second, where one of his legs is maimed

Dwapara: The third, where two of his legs are disabled

Kali: The last, where Dharma is said to limp on just one leg

Namita Gokhale is a multi-faceted Indian novelist and publisher, and the author of *Paro: Dreams of Passion* (1984), *Gods, Graves and Grandmother* (1994), *A Himalayan Love Story* (1996), *The Book of Shadows* (1999), *The Book of Shiva* (2001) and *Shakuntala: The play of Memory* (2005), all published by Penguin India. In her forthcoming anthology *In Search of Sita*, she re-examines the figure of Sita in both mythic and modern contexts.

The Puffin Mahabharata is her first book for young readers.

Suddhasattwa Basu is a painter, illustrator and animation film-maker, who studied at the College of Art, Calcutta. He is one of India's foremost illustrators of children's books. Among the books he has illustrated and designed are Khushwant Singh's *Nature Watch*, Ruskin Bond's *To Live in Magic* and V. Sulaiman's *The Homecoming*. He has also authored and illustrated a children's book *The Song of a Scarecrow* (Katha), for which he received the Chitrakatha Award 2003 for best children's book illustrations. He lives in Delhi and works under the banner of his company Raikhik Films.